Ministry of Culture, Government of the State of São Paulo, through the Secretariat of Culture, Creative Economy and Industry, Municipal Secretariat of Culture and Creative Economy of the City of São Paulo, Fundação Bienal de São Paulo and Itaú present

Not All Travellers Walk Roads

36th Bienal de São Paulo

Of Humanity as Practice

bienal

Browse our YouTube channel and check out the documentation of the *Invocation #4*.

Educational Publication

Vol. 4

Bukimi no Tani (不気味の谷):

The Uncanny Valley –

The Affectivity of the Humanoid

Since 1953, the year of its second edition, the Bienal de São Paulo has stood out for its educational commitment, promoting initiatives that facilitate access to exhibition content for diverse audiences – including teachers, students, and educators. In 2009, the Fundação Bienal established a permanent education team that has since been developing and implementing educational projects for each edition. These projects include publications, guided visits, workshops, and training programs for teachers and educators, all aimed at fulfilling the Fundação Bienal's mission of expanding access to contemporary art.

For the 36th Bienal de São Paulo – *Not All Travellers Walk Roads – Of Humanity as Practice*, the Fundação presents a series of four educational publications with two complementary objectives, both of fundamental importance to the Bienal. The first is to document and share the contributions of the *Invocations* – curatorial gatherings with artists and poets that explore notions of humanity, the exhibition's central theme, through the lens of four distinct geographies: Marrakech, Guadeloupe, Zanzibar, and Tokyo. The second objective is to support the educational project of the 36th Bienal, with these books serving as key resources in the training of mediators and in outreach activities, both during the months of preparation and execution of the exhibition and throughout the traveling exhibitions program that will follow.

As is characteristic of the Bienal de São Paulo, the content of these publications weaves together local and global perspectives, addressing contemporary practices and issues. The result of a partnership with the Center for Art, Research and Alliances (CARA), which co-published the books with the Fundação Bienal, and the A&L Berg Foundation, which supported the project from the outset, these educational publications are now available in English and will be distributed internationally for the first time, expanding the reach of the *Invocations* and our educational content, and reaffirming the Bienal's international vocation, which has been continuously enacted for over seventy years.

Andrea Pinheiro
President – Fundação Bienal de São Paulo

CARA is thrilled to co-produce this publication with the Bienal de São Paulo, reinforcing our shared commitment to expanding spaces for artistic and intellectual inquiry. The *Invocations* programs and these four educational volumes echo CARA's dedication to publishing as an act of transformation – where knowledge is not just recorded but activated through encounters across disciplines and geographies. Our institutional approach fosters open-ended research, challenges fixed narratives, and embraces storytelling as a means of keeping ideas in motion, unsettling dominant histories, and opening pathways for unlearning.

Building on this ethos, CARA's publishing program amplifies overlooked voices, supporting elder and mid-career practitioners and alternative historiographies. Our books embrace literary and poetic practices; visual, moving-image, and performance art; and radical action as entangled forces shaping how we understand our interconnected worlds. Through the *Invocations* series, CARA furthers its commitment to publishing as a space of resonance – where artistic and intellectual work resists singular narratives. This collaboration with the 36th Bienal de São Paulo strengthens our mission to amplify artists, scholars, and cultural workers whose contributions shape critical discourse, foster new connections, and expand the boundaries of thought.

At CARA, we ask: How can we dream not only about ourselves? This question guides our editorial vision, inviting us to create spaces where knowledge is shared and deepened in dynamic relation. For us, publishing is a process of bringing into generative constellation – where voices converge, entangle, and expand what can be imagined together. This collaboration embodies that ethos, offering books that challenge, unsettle, and inspire new ways of thinking and being in the world.

Manuela Moscoso
Executive and Artistic Director – CARA

The A&L Berg Foundation, founded in 2023 by Allison and Larry Berg, provides access, tools and resources to create, evolve and sustain diverse perspectives and narratives in the United States visual arts. We support and empower individuals committed to making systemic and scalable impact in their practices and communities.

The Foundation's core program is the ESAP Fellowship, which supports and empowers early stage visual arts curators, educators and administrators working in United States arts spaces and institutions. Through building a long-lasting peer support system, and providing navigational tools and opportunities to create expanded professional networks and communities, the Foundation creates equitable visual arts career pathways and ultimately aims to strengthen and diversify the internal ecosystems of United States art institutions.

Our programs provide access to networks, professional development workshops, international research travel, mentorship, relational and soft skills coaching, and financial support for navigating systemic inequities. Each year, a different jury of esteemed arts professionals nominates candidates based on an agreed upon set of criteria, and we invite six of those individuals to participate in the fellowship cohort. Our guest program director, an arts professional who has already successfully navigated the challenges facing the respective cohort, designs the annual program details with a focus on the relational skills that specific cohort requires for career growth.

During the ten-month fellowship, the Foundation provides five empowerment prongs: mentorship with a more established arts professional; relational skills workshops with specialists spanning a variety of industries; an unrestricted financial grant; a robust international research trip opening doors and offering engagement with visual art leaders and peers from every part of the global art ecosystem and ongoing support for professional growth.

A&L Berg Foundation

The Fundação Bienal de São Paulo thanks its partners CARA and A&L Berg Foundation for their special collaboration on the educational publications of the 36th Bienal.

The Federal Government, through the Ministry of Culture, is celebrating the 36th Bienal de São Paulo in partnership with the Fundação Bienal de São Paulo. Just like the great film festivals, the Bienal de São Paulo – the second oldest art biennial in the world – raises enormous expectations on the global exhibition circuit. This year, with the title *Not All Travellers Walk Roads – Of Humanity as Practice*, inspired by a poem by the renowned Brazilian writer Conceição Evaristo, the Bienal reaffirms its vocation as a major showcase for the most current production on the national and global art scene, without losing sight of its wide-ranging educational activities in the formation of new and well-known audiences.

The Ministry of Culture has been working to strengthen the cultural sector through various initiatives and promotion tools. Policies such as the Paulo Gustavo Law and the Aldir Blanc National Policy for the Promotion of Culture encourage other artistic languages, creating opportunities for artists, cultural producers, managers, and visitors. Creating solid conditions for culture means strengthening the creative economy and encouraging the implementation of perennial, permanent, and democratic cultural policies.

Being alongside projects like the Bienal's new movie theater is a source of pride, as it brings together two issues dear to the government: expanding democratic access to cultural facilities combined with an educational arm capable of mediating and making sense of what is on display. By providing free film screenings accompanied by educational activities, another stage is created to strengthen the culture of our country's award-winning and increasingly active audiovisual field.

The Federal Government remains committed to arts and education, which are indispensable fronts for ensuring the right to citizenship and a fairer future for all. We will continue to invest in initiatives that encourage cultural creation and innovation, ensuring that events such as the Bienal de São Paulo continue to inspire and transform generations.

Margareth Menezes
Minister of Culture – Federal Government of Brazil

For more than 35 years, Itaú Cultural (IC) has played a fundamental role in boosting the appreciation of art, culture and education in a complex and heterogeneous society like Brazil. This role is expanded through essential partners for the development of the cultural and creative economy, such as the Fundação Bienal de São Paulo.

Itaú Unibanco is proud to be a sponsor of the Fundação Bienal de São Paulo – it has been for the past 27 years, with this being the 12th edition held in that period – reaffirming its commitment to promoting the visual arts and their transformative role. The Bienal de São Paulo is an important meeting and exchange space for artists, curators, critics, and the public.

In this field, Itaú Cultural organizes actions for enjoyment, education and promotion, including solo and group exhibitions that take place both at its headquarters on Avenida Paulista, 149 (with free admission) and at venues in Brazil's five regions. Highlights of the 2025 exhibitions include *Carlos Zilio – A querela do Brasil*, curated by Paulo Miyada, which will present a retrospective of this artist who, with erudition and irreverence, explored the tensions of Brazilian art. Exhibitions will also be dedicated to the visual artist Rivane Neuenschwander and the curator and critic Paulo Herkenhoff.

Visit itaucultural.org.br to browse the *Filmes e vídeos de artistas* virtual exhibitions, with experimental audiovisual works, and *Livros de artista na Coleção Itaú Cultural*, whose immersive and interactive features allow for detailed appreciation. At Enciclopédia Itaú Cultural (enciclopedia. itaucultural.org.br) you can access hundreds of entries on figures, works, and events in the visual arts.

Being present at the Bienal de São Paulo reinforces our goal of building links with different audiences, valuing the diversity of formats, thoughts, and subjectivities, and fostering creative and critical thinking through Brazilian art and culture.

Itaú Cultural

Bloomberg is proud to sponsor of the 36th edition of the Bienal de São Paulo. For more than a decade we have supported the Bienal's exceptional contemporary art exhibitions in the stunning Ciccillo Matarazzo Pavilion in Ibirapuera Park and around Brazil, through our partnership with Fundação Bienal. This year's edition continues the tradition of presenting captivating and thought-provoking art installations that are free and open to the public.

Every day, Bloomberg connects influential decision makers to a dynamic network of information, people, and ideas. With more than 19,000 employees in 176 offices, Bloomberg delivers business and financial information, news and insight around the world. Our dedication to innovation and new ideas extends to our longstanding support of arts, which we believe are a valuable way to engage citizens and strengthen communities. Through our funding, we help increase access to culture and empower artists and cultural organizations to reach broader audiences.

Bloomberg

For Bradesco, a Brazilian bank *par excellence* that has just celebrated its 83rd anniversary, art and culture are not only fundamental elements in the formation of a people's identity or the construction of their intangible heritage, but also a journey of inclusion and citizenship, a healthy convergence of different points of view. It is, so to speak, a journey towards the new, but with the care to value what is special enough to be history or tradition.

Therefore, when it comes to art and culture, the boundaries between past, present, and future, between form and content, become meaningless. Everything becomes reflection and learning, everything becomes provocation and surprise.

It was on the basis of this interpretation, combined with the positive view of the role of companies in making possible what society considers important, that Bradesco became a sponsor of the 36th edition of the Bienal de São Paulo, undoubtedly one of the most important events in the country aimed at promoting the arts scene, publicizing the various expressions of art and promoting cultural exchange, with all the good that this brings.

By participating in something that is both great and multifaceted, Bradesco shares with the Fundação Bienal de São Paulo – which has organized the event for more than six decades – the goal of democratizing access to culture, multiplying its reach and promoting the appreciation of art.

It's a path with no end, no turning back, full of challenges and at least one certainty: the more people who take part, the better!

Bradesco

Petrobras has a history of more than forty years of continuously believing in culture as a transformational element and a source of energy for society. By supporting unique projects and long-term partnerships, we have built a relationship of respect and collaboration with producers and initiatives all over the country.

The Petrobras Cultural Program has Brazilianness as its guiding element, which is materialized in the themes, origins, curatorship, history, and characteristics of each project we select. By supporting different projects, we put into practice our belief that culture is an important energy that transforms society. We believe that through creativity and inspiration we promote growth and change.

The Bienal de São Paulo is one of the sector's most prestigious events in the country and the world. Petrobras's sponsorship reinforces the company's role in promoting culture in its various forms, consolidating its position as one of the biggest supporters of the arts in Brazil.

Events such as the Bienal de São Paulo make a significant contribution to the economy, promoting innovation, creativity, and sustainability in the economic dynamic. Petrobras is an ally of Brazil's development in its various sectors. It invests in many forms of energy, and culture is certainly one of them.

Petrobras is proud to support Brazilian culture in its plurality of manifestations, taking art to all audiences, all over the country. Because culture is also our energy.

To find out more about the Petrobras Cultural Program, visit petrobras.com.br/cultura.

Petrobras

Instituto Vale Cultural believes in the transformative power of culture. As one of the main supporters of culture in Brazil, it sponsors and promotes projects that foster connections between people, initiatives, and territories. Its commitment is to make culture increasingly accessible and diverse, while also contributing to the strengthening of the creative economy.

It is therefore a pleasure to be part of the realization of this 36th Bienal de São Paulo and its educational program, which explores new formats and approaches. Developed from the *Invocations* proposed by the curatorial team – encounters with poetry, music, performance, and debates that explore notions of humanity across different geographies – the educational program expands the Bienal's communication with diverse audiences and extends its reach beyond the exhibition space and timeframe, in an interdisciplinary way.

With each new edition, the Bienal invites us to rethink art as an exercise in dialogue, in openness to new narratives, and as a space for learning. In this sense, it aligns with the purpose of the Instituto Cultural Vale: to expand opportunities for learning, reflection, new perspectives, and the sharing of art, culture, and education – both inside and outside museums, throughout Brazil.

Where there is culture, Vale is there.

Instituto Cultural Vale

For 110 years, Citi has been part of Brazil's history, accompanying its transformations and driving its development. Our journey is intertwined with that of the country: we are both witnesses to and participants in a Brazil that constantly reinvents itself and moves forward.

More than a financial institution, we believe in the power of culture and education as engines for a more inclusive, innovative, and sustainable future. Investing in these pillars also means celebrating the diversity, creativity, and talent that define the Brazilian spirit.

With this commitment, we are proud, for the first time, to support the 36th Bienal de São Paulo – one of the most important spaces for artistic expression in Latin America, where Brazil thinks, feels, and reinvents itself through art.

We believe in art as an agent of social transformation. Artistic creation has the power to spark dialogue, expand horizons, and inspire new possibilities for the world. By sponsoring the Bienal, we reaffirm our commitment to culture, innovation, and all those who, through art, are building new narratives for both the present and the future.

Citi

Vivo believes in culture as a means of social transformation and is one of the most important brands supporting the visual and performing arts and music in Brazil. Art, like technology, creates connections between people and encourages the search for balance between history, nature and time.

Vivo is currently a sponsor of the most important museums in Brazil, such as the Museu de Arte de São Paulo Assis Chateaubriand (MASP), the Pinacoteca de São Paulo, the Museu da Imagem e do Som (MIS-São Paulo), the Museu Afro Brasil Emanoel Araujo, the Museu de Arte Moderna de São Paulo (MAM SP), as well as the Instituto Inhotim and the Palácio das Artes, both in Minas Gerais, and the Museu Oscar Niemeyer, in Paraná.

Teatro Vivo, located in São Paulo, offers a curated selection of contemporary plays that promote reflection on current issues and value cultural diversity. In addition, it is a fully accessible space, offering resources such as translation into Libras (Brazilian sign language), audio descriptions and trained staff, ensuring inclusion for people with disabilities and reduced mobility. In 2024, it welcomed over 50,000 people.

The brand also supports projects in the world of music that are genuinely Brazilian and regional, reinforcing its proximity with local culture at iconic and traditional events in our country, such as the Parintins Festival, Galo da Madrugada, the Çairé Festival, Lollapalooza, The Town, and Vivo Música.

The brand's initiatives in the cultural sphere broaden access to knowledge with new ways of experiencing and learning, strengthened by the aspects of diversity, sustainability, inclusion and education. All information is gathered and shared on the @vivo.cultura and @vivo Instagram profiles.

Vivo

Confronted with the incessant problems of humanity, perhaps it is worth dwelling a little longer on some open questions, taking sustenance from resources that allow us to dig and build answers procedurally. In this sense, art, in its many guises, offers fertile ground for critical elaborations about the world and ourselves.

The meeting of art and education – both understood as fields of knowledge – enables the torsion of time and space: it becomes possible, thus, to suspend neutralities and dilate what is precipitated in structures. How far is this approach able to infer the real and interfere in it? It allows us to (re)populate imaginaries, to unpick the universalizing statute attributed to concepts, practices and people, and thus to carve out reality with narratives that articulate the individual and the collective, in a procedural and coherent manner regarding the issues that permeate existence.

It is according to this panorama that Sesc São Paulo and the Fundação Bienal, through the 35th Bienal de São Paulo, reiterate their long-standing partnership, a mutual commitment to fostering experiences of coexistence with the visual arts, expanding access to cultural actions and the exercise of otherness.

This partnership, which has been established and renewed for over a decade, has led to the promotion of projects such as simultaneous exhibitions, public meetings, seminars and training for educators, as well as the consolidated itinerant exhibition with excerpts from the Bienal in Sesc units in the wider state of São Paulo. The confluence of choices and propositions is part of the institutional perspective of culture as a right, and conceives, together with one of the largest exhibitions in the country, an accessible horizon for contemporary art in Brazil.

Sesc São Paulo

Foreword
Fundação Bienal de São Paulo

This book is an extension of the investigations into notions of humanity in different parts of the world, in dialogue with the ideas of the 36th Bienal de São Paulo *Not All Travelers Walk Roads – Of Humanity as Practice* based on its fourth and final *Invocation, Bukimi No Tani (不気味の谷): The Uncanny Valley – The Affectivity of the Humanoid,* which took place in Tokyo in April 2025.

The *Invocations* were meetings with poetry, research, music, and dance performances that preceded the exhibition in São Paulo. In addition to Tokyo, they took place in three other territories: Marrakech, Guadeloupe, and Zanzibar, between November 2024 and April 2025.

23

So what can be done to avoid sinking into the chronic
depression that paralyzes citizens? Is there any way
to restore the city's spirit / de-lobotomize / recharge its
batteries? Simple: just inject a little energy into the mud and
stimulate what fertility remains in the veins of Recife.[1]

Written in 1992, the "Caranguejos com cérebro" [Crabs With Brains] manifesto presented the proposals of Manguebeat and paved the way for the
movement, which emerged on the streets of Recife, to bring new perspectives to the Brazilian cultural scene in the final decade of the 20th century.
With the symbolism of an antenna rising from the mud, the mangueboys'
and manguegirls' response to the various crises in the country was rela-
tively simple: "to allegorically connect the good vibrations of the mangroves
with the worldwide circulation of pop concepts."[2]

Since the 1990s, the possibilities and understandings of "connection," as well as the circulation of information and affections mediated
by technology, have undergone major transformations. The interconnec-
tion of devices to a global communication network and the development
of machines capable of learning, making decisions, and interacting in
increasingly intimate ways with humans have not only changed our relationship with technology but also challenge us to reflect on what defines us
as humanity.

Invocation #4 explored the complex relationship between
humans and machines through sound, performance, and visual practices.
Inspired by the concept of the "Uncanny Valley," proposed by Japanese
roboticist Masahiro Mori (1927–2025) in an essay published in 1970,[3] the
Tokyo *Invocation* reflected on the ambiguities of the human in the face
of technology and the issues that emerge at the intersection of art, artificial intelligence, the body, and affectivity. Held from April 12 to 14, 2025,
the event addressed topics such as the impact of artificial intelligence
on artistic creation processes, the presence of machines in cultural life,
and the affective dimensions of relationships between human beings and
automated devices.

This publication, in addition to documenting the talks, conversations, and performances presented during *Invocation* #4, offers content
that expands upon the ideas raised during the event, aiming to bring its
discussions closer to other geographies and realities, with a particular
focus on the Brazilian educational context. The possibilities, contradictions, and strangeness of the contemporary world arising from
the encounters between humans and machines form a vast field of

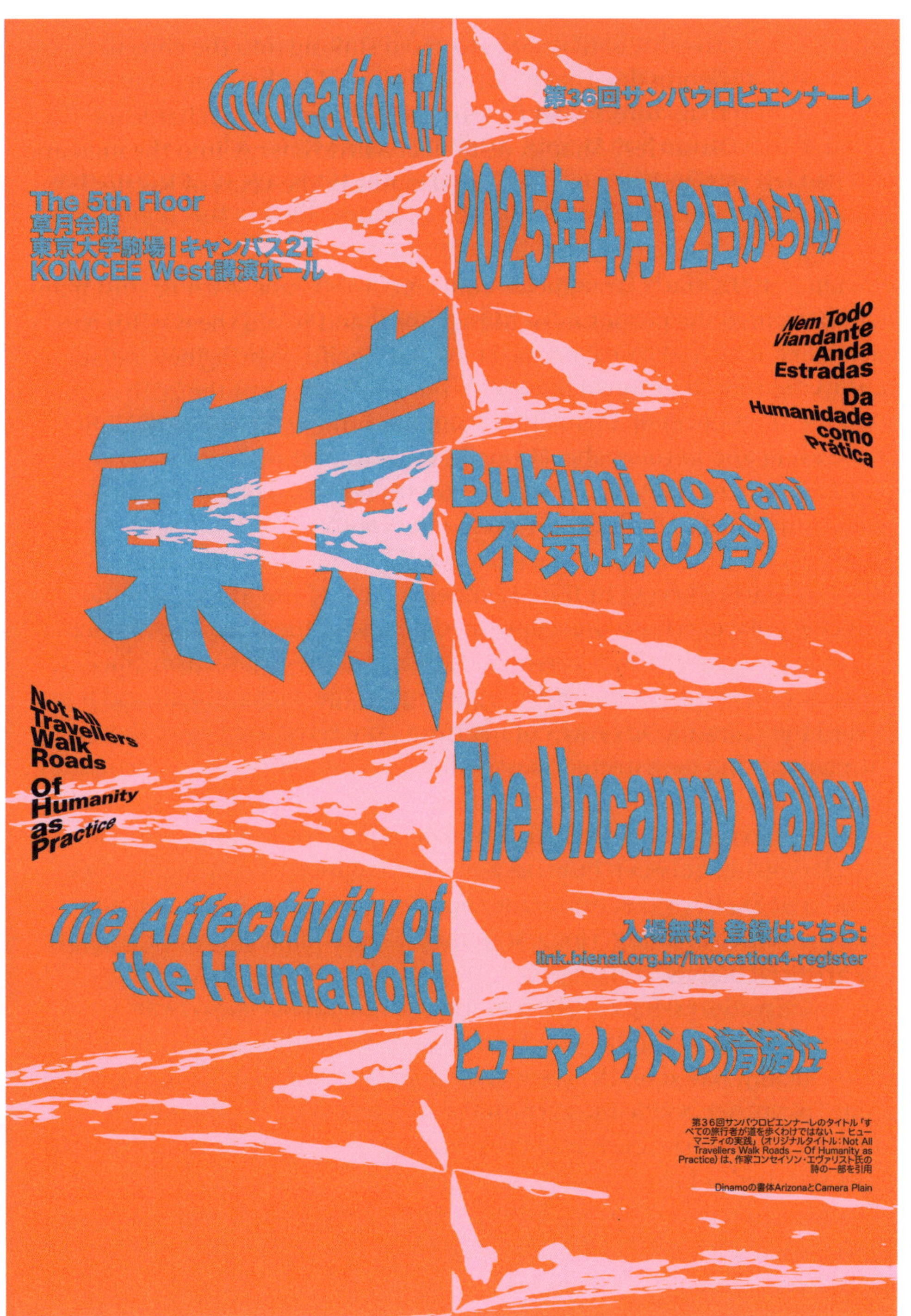
Invocation #4
第36回サンパウロビエンナーレ
The 5th Floor
草月会館
東京大学駒場Iキャンパス21
KOMCEE West講演ホール
2025年4月12日から14日
Nem Todo Viandante Anda Estradas Da Humanidade como Prática
東京
Bukimi no Tani
(不気味の谷)
Not All Travellers Walk Roads Of Humanity as Practice
The Uncanny Valley
The Affectivity of the Humanoid
入場無料 登録はこちら:
link.bienal.org.br/invocation4-register
ヒューマノイドの情動性
第36回サンパウロビエンナーレのタイトル「すべての旅行者が道を歩くわけではない ─ ヒューマニティの実践」(オリジナルタイトル：Not All Travellers Walk Roads ─ Of Humanity as Practice) は、作家コンセイソン・エヴァリスト氏の詩の一部を引用
Dinamoの書体ArizonaとCamera Plain

inquiry – from the thinking of Masahiro Mori to the experiments of poets, artists, and intellectuals.

At the opening of the *Invocation*, the chief curator of the 36th Bienal, Bonaventure Soh Bejeng Ndikung, read a letter addressed to Mori, who had left our (increasingly uncanny) world at the age of 98, just a few months before the gathering. In the letter, transcribed in this publication, Ndikung poses a question directly connected to the Japanese scientist's thought – particularly his interest in the movements of empathy and repulsion that people feel toward machines: how does our species, so often incapable of valuing and recognizing the humanity of fellow human beings, venture into the creation of humanoid robots?

This question resonates throughout the various interventions of the event and in this publication. In her text "Her Rights: *The Turk of Frankenstein*; or, *The Modern Prometheus*," visual artist and poet Natsumi Aoyagi imagines a confluence between the creations of Wolfgang von Kempelen (1734–1804) and Mary Shelley (1797–1851). In order to entertain Empress Maria Theresa in 1770, Kempelen created the "Turk," an automaton chess player whose skill captivated people at the time, even though it was secretly operated by a person hidden inside the mechanism. Shelley, in her novel *Frankenstein* (1818), reflecting on the enchantment and fear toward the scientific advances of her time, conceived a creature that was both human and monstrous, questioning the boundaries between natural and artificial. Her work captured a disquiet that has spanned centuries, inviting us to reflect on the ethical and emotional dilemmas surrounding the relationship between humans and their creations. Both Kempelen's "Turk" and Shelley's creature stage the boundary between human and machine while revealing a long-standing fascination and unease with lifelike artificial beings.

In addressing the preservation of life, artist Asako Iwama explores perceptions related to food production both aesthetically and epistemologically, based on the resonance of nature within human subjectivity. From Tokyo, her poetic intervention recalls that some 5,500 miles away, in Berlin – where she currently lives and works –, all the bees contracted a virus and died, a fact rarely discussed, much like the deaths of thousands of Palestinians in the conflict with Israel. For her, in Germany – a country whose traumatic past has fostered a culture of memory – little is remembered about the death of the bees or the genocide in Gaza.

Meanwhile, the Noh theater play *Irumagawa*, by multimedia artist Shiori Watanabe, in collaboration with performers Shingo Kato and Noboru Yasuda and computer researcher Dominique Chen, investigates the interrelationships between nature, humans, other

26

beings, and ecological and political systems. The play turns the Emperor of Japan into an allegory to address the ideological contradictions that permeate contemporary Japanese society. Both Watanabe and Iwama reveal how environmental and humanitarian crises are silenced or forgotten and propose poetic and critical ways of reinscribing these themes into sensitive experience. By bringing life, art, and technology together, they invite us to question erasures and rethink our ethical responsibilities in an increasingly interconnected world.

The relationship between ethical consumption and aesthetic production as elements that mobilize the fashion world brings together two conversations held during the *Invocation* and documented here: the dialogue between T-Michael and the chief curator of the 36th Bienal de São Paulo, and Manauara Clandestina's exchange with the Bienal team. With a conceptual approach to men's tailoring, T-Michael, in conversation with Bonaventure Soh Bejeng Ndikung, discusses the relationship between body and clothing, understanding dressing as a form of self-expression deeply tied to subjectivity, while addressing issues such as the pricing and sustainability. Manauara Clandestina, whose practice involves the reuse of discarded materials, transforming what society considers waste into new garments with different meanings and concepts, shares her perspective on upcycling technology as a way to address social issues such as the neglect of marginalized bodies and the unsustainable consumption patterns of traditional fashion.

In an effort to bring the discussions of *Invocation* #4 closer to the classroom realities, we present transcribed and edited versions of lessons given by specialists for the Bienal team. In "Demystifying AI: History, Techniques, and Considerations," anti-racist hacker Nina da Hora provides a historical reflection on the development of artificial intelligence, imagining new horizons for the relationship between technology and education. Professor Deivison Faustino, examining the relationship between humanity, technology, and affectivity, brings the "Uncanny Valley" closer to the so-called Eliza effect,[4] offering a critical perspective on the encounters and contradictions revealed in these technological crossings, which – far from being neutral – often reinforce colonial logics and structures of servitude, reprogramming oppression and means of exploitation.

In Lynn Hershman Leeson's dialogue with co-curator Anna Roberta Goetz and in Gê Viana's conversation with the Bienal team, the relationship between technology, art, and community life is approached from different angles. Through digital collages and an understanding of the Tambor de Mina as an ancestral technology, Gê Viana proposes the exercise of "remixing the image" as a way to recreate memories and generate new narratives about Afro-Indigenous communities. In her research, Viana shares narratives gathered during her travels to the Indigenous and *quilombola* territories in Maranhão, revealing an alternative understanding of technology: listening to people. highlighting the wisdom of figures such as Dona Miúda, a resident of Alcântara – home to one of Brazil's two rocket launch centers –, Viana presents a wordview that far surpasses space technology. In turn, the conversation with Lynn Hershman Leeson discusses the social impact of the internet, public fears surrounding new technologies, and the collection of personal data, based on her works *Agent Ruby* (1998–) and *Dina* (2004), addressing the reception of these projects that pioneered the use of chatbots and artificial intelligence, decades before the commercial use of these tools in today's devices. In this publication, the conversation, originally carried out through an email exchange, appears in the style of an instant messaging chat, in an exercise that brings the content of the discussion closer to the aesthetics of this mode of communication that is so present in everyday life.

Reflecting on the near-omnipresence of technology in our daily lives, Yale professor Tavia Nyong'o was invited to revisit the ideas presented in the chapter "Chore and Choice" from his book *Afro-Fabulations: The Queer Drama of Black Life*[5] during *Invocation* #4. In the book, his central argument is that Masahiro Mori's notion of the "Uncanny Valley" has been profoundly transformed since its original formulation in 1970. For Nyong'o, the "Valley" is no longer an occasional exception – a state humanity slips into whenever faced with a technological device that fails to generate empathy – but rather the environment in which we now live. Daily life is populated by technologies and interfaces that excessively mirror us, attempting to anticipate and imitate us in a more or less crude way. The "Uncanny" has ceased to be a rupture in ordinary life and has become a continuous state.

In his 2018 work, Nyong'o imagined a depressed Black cyborg, inspired by the real-life story of Bina48, a social android created in 2010 using artificial intelligence built from the memories, attitudes, beliefs, and mannerisms of a human interlocutor. For Nyong'o, the figure of a depressed Black cyborg was a way to address failure – not as lack, but as resistance to what he calls a "compulsory future." At the time, the author's aim was to find a poetics of failure, a choreography of refusal. Almost a decade later, revisiting this work in the Tokyo *Invocation*, the author gave the cyborg the traits of an anxious personality: someone mourning something she cannot name, whose deepest unease lies in the growing awareness that the world we live in is already an Uncanny Valley. Far from predicting the future, this cyborg speaks of our present and is already among us – in the algorithm that anticipates desire, in the voice assistant that misreads intonation, and in the feedback loops of overwork and under-knowledge. In both his talk and the reworked transcription published here, Nyong'o presents the "Manifesto of the Anxious Cyborg."

From there we return to the "Crabs with Brains" manifesto, understood as the documentation of a *moving scene* and as a *narrated memory*[6] of Recife's cultural effervescence, whose fertile mud has fostered various artistic manifestations. This perspective also informed the practices of the creative laboratories for this educational publication of the 36th Bienal de São Paulo, seeking to bring the exhibition's themes closer to educational contexts through languages such as music, literature, and cinema. For this final volume, we were inspired by human-machine relations, using sounds, images, and narratives as tools to promote encounters and imagine new realities, once again connecting Tokyo Bay and the Capibaribe River in the ongoing quest to bring humanity together.

1   The "Caranguejos com cérebro" [Crabs with Brains] manifesto was written by Fred Zeroquatro and Renato Lins and widely distributed in 1992. It is considered the founding manifesto of the Manguebeat movement. For more information, see https://jornaldigital.recife.br/2023/03/30/manguebeat-inovacao-cultural-do-recife-para-o-mundo/. Accessed in May 2025.

2   Ibid.

3   Masahiro Mori, "The Uncanny Valley: The Original Essay by Masahiro Mori." *IEEE Spectrum*, June 12, 2012. Available at https://spectrum.ieee.org/the-uncanny-valley. Accessed in May 2025.

4   In computer science, the Eliza effect refers to the tendency to attribute human capacities – such as understanding or empathy – to computer programs with a textual interface. This is a category error in which the manipulation of texts based on formal rules is interpreted as if it involved mental processes such as "thinking," "knowing," or "understanding."

5   Tavia Nyong'o, *Afro-Fabulations: The Queer Drama of Black Life*. New York: New York University Press, 2018.

6   Reference to "Moving Scene" and "Narrated Memory," titles of the "Educational Activities" of this educational publication, pp. 116–125 of this volume.

A Letter to Professor Masahiro Mori

Bonaventure Soh Bejeng Ndikung

Reproduction of the opening speech
delivered in Tokyo on April 12, 2025.

Dear Professor Masahiro Mori,

It's been a long time that I have been meaning to write you this letter.
As they say, "procrastination is the thief of time." So instead of beginning
this letter with "I trust this letter finds you well and in good spirits," now I
have to write "I trust your soul is resting well and in good spirits."

In my imagination, I had seen us making a toast with some sake.
Now I will pour some sake as a libation in your honor.

It was only a few weeks ago that we learned that on the 12th of
January, 2025, you transitioned to the greater beyond. It came as a surprise
to many of us, even though you were only two years shy of a hundred.
Somehow many of us were convinced you were going to live forever.
And somehow, even though you are no longer physically with us, I am
convinced you will be with us forever. This gathering here in Tokyo that
was prompted by your concept of the "Uncanny Valley" is testament to that.

You must be asking yourself why all these people are here in
Tokyo in the name of the Bienal de São Paulo. Or what the Bienal de
São Paulo has to do with you and why we have chosen Tokyo as a destination for its *Invocations*. Don't worry, I can assure you that you are not the
only one asking these questions.

Until now, when asked how Tokyo aligns with Marrakesh,
Guadeloupe, and Zanzibar in this *Invocation* trajectory, I have always given
people the pres-kit version of the story, namely:

1) The importance of water to all lives at large and to humanity in particular: I have explained to people that Marrakesh's connection to the
Mediterranean Sea, Guadeloupe's location at the Atlantic Ocean, Zanzibar's
position at the Afro-Asian Ocean (aka the Indian Ocean), and Tokyo's place
on the Pacific Ocean were key reasons for us to do the mapping for the
Invocations.

2) The importance of the sonic and of performativity at large, and of music
in particular: it was the divine beauty of Gnawa music that drew us to
Marrakesh; in Guadeloupe, the enchantment of Gwoka music put a spell on
us; in Zanzibar, the magic of Taarab music captivated us; and in
Tokyo, we expect to be beguiled by the music of the *hayashi* and

their *shibyōshi* in Noh theater, as well as by the way you relate to Bunraku in your practice.[1]

3) Then there was the argument that, if the goal of the 36th edition was to conjugate humanity, we needed to experience how different societies across the globe engage in that conjugation in their daily lives, and how artists and other practitioners around the world could help make the conjugation of humanity felt by giving it form.

So here we are in Tokyo under the auspices of your concept of the "Uncanny Valley" for which I have more questions than answers, dear Professor Mori. But before I burden you with my understandings and misunderstandings of your concept, I would like to confide in you that one of the key reasons why I personally wanted to be here, within the framework of the Bienal de São Paulo – whose subtitle is "Humanity as a Practice," – is something you said in a 2012 interview with Norri Kageki for *IEEE Spectrum* magazine. In that interview you said you were working

> on the relationship between technology and the teachings of Buddha. To develop robots, you need to understand humans. I think the teachings of Buddha is the best way to understand humans, especially with regard to understanding the human mind.[2]

For me, this is the main reason we are here: to learn from you and others about what it means to be human in our current times, and how that could guide us in the technologies and mediums we create to mediate between human beings and the world. To learn from you and others about the relationships between technology and spirituality. To learn from you and others how spirituality can help us comprehend the complexities of the human mind.

I still remember how dumbfounded I was when I first read your essay "The Uncanny Valley,"[3] originally published in the Japanese journal *Energy* in 1970, seven years before I came into this world. The essay came out just a few months after an interim military junta seized power in Brazil (August to October, 1969), soon followed by Emílio Garrastazu Médici, whose government (1969–1974) represented the apex of Brazil's military regime. Thus, your essay came out at a time when humans were not only making humanoids, but had transformed themselves into varying forms of humanoids through military machinations. So your essay came out between the 10th Bienal, which took place in 1969, and the

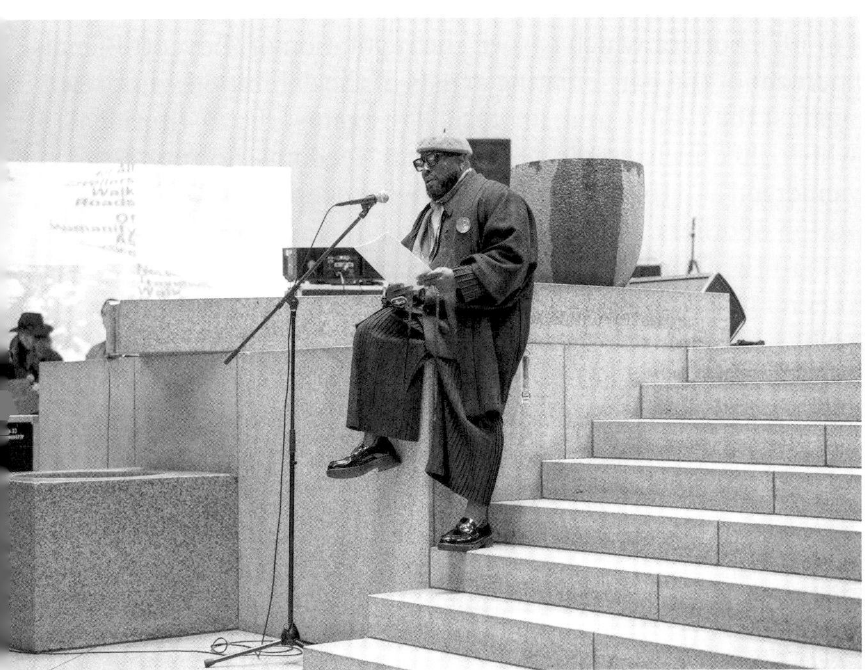

© Naoki Takehisa / Fundação Bienal de São Paulo

11th Bienal in 1971, both of which earned the reputation of "boycott Bienals," as over 80 percent of the participating artists of the exhibition withdrew in protest against the regime and, in particular, against the Institutional Act no. 5, which effectively eradicated personal freedoms. So your essay poignantly emerged at a time when humans were deeply engaged in the dehumanization of others. Therefore, how can humans who cannot even value the humanity of other humans create humanoid robots?

When I first read your essay about a decade ago, I remember wondering why such a sharp reflection on human behavior and affectivity didn't catch more attention back in 1970. But I was equally amazed by how your proposal has reverberated not only within robotics design but also across science, technology, and art circles in the subsequent decades since. So if you like, we are here because the ripples from "The Uncanny Valley" stone you threw into the water in 1970 are still spreading across the globe.

Toward the end of your essay, you posed some crucial questions – questions deeply relevant to our gathering here, when you asked:

> Why were we equipped with this eerie sensation [of the Uncanny Valley]? Is it essential for human beings? I have not yet considered these questions deeply, but I have no doubt it is an integral part of our instinct for self-preservation." You went on to write that "we should begin to build an accurate map of the Uncanny Valley, so that through robotics research we can come to understand what makes us human.

This quest to understand what makes us human by studying robots continues to amaze me and lies at the crux of our *Invocation* here – a relationship you illustrated brilliantly through your graph of affinity versus human likeness. It is a profound revelation about affect in representation, both on the side of the subject (the human) and even more so on the side of the object (the robot). As you wrote: "I have noticed that, in climbing toward the goal of making robots appear human, our affinity for them increases until we come to a valley, which I call the *Uncanny Valley*." In other words, the closer the mirror image comes to reality, the greater the sense of unease, and the stronger the fear of being deceived and betrayed.

Making robots is one thing – and very few of us will ever have the chance to make robots in our lives –, but the experience you describe is something I understand all too well. For me, it doesn't even have to be a robot. That eerie feeling arises even when I see a wax figure of David Beckham or some other prominent figure at Madame Tussauds. The uncanny similarity, the coldness in the eyes, the corpse-like quality of the wax figures freak me out… and too often, it feels like Beckham might suddenly take off running – which makes it even spookier. This is the association I made between the Uncanny Valley and movement. The example you give in your essay makes this picture drives the point home even more, when you write:

> Since negative effects of movement are apparent even with a prosthetic hand, a whole robot would magnify the creepiness. And that is just one robot. Imagine a craftsman being awakened suddenly in the dead of night. He searches downstairs for something among a crowd of mannequins in his workshop. If the mannequins started to move, it would be like a horror story.

Dear Professor Mori, in rereading your essay for this Invocation, and anticipating meeting you, I found my mind flooded with questions about human-robot relationships and affect. One thing that stood out was our tendency to humanize all forms of robots, even those with little human-specific features – something that brings me to the lower left corner of your graph, where industrial robots sit with both low affinity and human likeness. Consider the recent trend among my friends: almost everyone has bought a robot vacuum cleaner. Each of these robots has been given a human name and is sometimes carried around with the same care as one might give to a child. Though the likeness here is not physical, I still feel an eeriness similar to that of the steep drop into the Uncanny Valley. I am also thinking of our relationship with digital voice assistants like Siri or Alexa that have become almost indispensable in our lives. Their voices have become affectionate and are as familiar as the voices of our children. In the scope of artificial intelligence today, we have even seen scammers use AI to recreate people's voices and impersonate them for committing banking fraud over the phone. The point is that while in 1970 the primary marker of human likeness might have been the physical appearance, today we must consider sonic, olfactory, haptic markers too. Does the Uncanny Valley, in your view, also encompass this dimension as well?

Dear Professor Mori, your paper focuses on the possible outcomes of humans making humanoid machines, which is to say humans making robots in their own image. I have been wondering about what the other direction would look like: machines "making"/cultivating humans that look like machines or humans "making"/cultivating other humans in the image of machines. I know this might sound far-fetched… but wasn't the transatlantic enslavement project – which, from 1514 to 1866, saw

35

the transportation of 12 million Africans to the Americas to work on plantations – a project of humans cultivating other humans and turning them into robots? I also think of the much-celebrated Industrial Revolution, which led to the transformation of agriculture and handicrafts-based economies into mechanized large-scale industries, semi-automated factory systems, as well as human-dependent machines and machine-dependent humans to attain more productivity and efficiency. And the two world wars of the 20th century, and all the wars going on now across the globe, in which humans are transformed into war machines, in which drones and other robots are used to eliminate people who, in the eyes of these drones and robots, are nothing but statistics. What about those people who dropped the atomic bombs on Hiroshima and Nagasaki, knowing all too well that there were women, children, men, animals, plants in those places? Isn't this part of the culture of humans cultivating other humans and turning them into machines?

I ask these questions to find out where and when exactly the uncanniness, the eeriness, the disgust arise when we reverse the direction. How steep is the affinity curve of the Uncanny Valley when we realize that it is the human who has become so similar to the machine? Or perhaps this comparison insults certain machines – machines that some might consider to have souls. What is the depth of the Uncanny Valley for soulless human-machines?

As you can see, dear Professor Mori, there are too many questions I wished to ask you, and I am hereby releasing them into the ether, hoping that you will find a way to answer me.

I would like to go back to the point in the interview where you said: "To develop robots, you need to understand humans." I must ask: Given all that is going on in the world right now, and what has been going on for the past 500 years or so, is it safe to say that we humans do not understand humanity? And if that is the case, and according to your analysis, can or should we continue to develop robots? Another way to phrase this: Have we lost so much of our humanity by investing too much in making robots human and too little in making humans more human? Essentially how do we conjugate humanity?

Returning to your original – and now almost classical – version of the Uncanny Valley. In your paper, you warned designers of the risk of falling into the valley:

> We hope to design and build robots and prosthetic hands that will not fall into the Uncanny Valley. Thus, because of the risk inherent in trying to increase their degree of

human likeness to scale the second peak, I recommend
that designers instead take the first peak as their goal,
which results in a moderate degree of human likeness and a
considerable sense of affinity. In fact, I predict it is possible
to create a safe level of affinity by deliberately pursuing a
nonhuman design. I ask designers to ponder this.

I now wonder how we got to the point where we have, for example, the
so-called Dutch-wife craze Japan, where the sex doll industry has produced
4,000-pound life-sized, hyper-real silicone female dolls, with realistic skin
and eyes, marketed as the perfect artificial girlfriend. Are these hyper-real
Dutch wives the exception that prove the rule within the context of the
Uncanny Valley? Why doesn't the eeriness kick in for the millions of men
who have acquired such dolls and for the many who have fallen in love
with them?

Dear Professor Mori, I still have a thousand and one questions to
ask you, but I also feel you have given us, in one way or another, a kind of
code with which we could answer at least some of them. When asked in the
aforementioned interview about those designers who aim for the other side
of the valley, you responded:

Using the woodcarving of a Buddha statue as an example,
that one last touch of the knife may destroy the whole thing.
There is a narrow margin for error.

I would like to take this statement as a crossroads between humanity, technology, and spirituality. I would like to see it as a reminder of the gentleness
and tact needed in the negotiations of that interface – between humanity,
technology, and spirituality. By the way, I think the German word for this,
Fingerspitzengefühl, though long, brings to the point what I mean, as it
translates as "fingertip feeling," sensitiveness, tact.

Yet we seem to be living in a world where people are using swords
and axes to carve Buddha statues. Clearly, we have a very long way to go
in weaving humanity, technology, and spirituality together. But it is time
to wake up and get this project moving while we reflect on how we can live
better in this world together. Or, as the legendary 17th-century Japanese
poet Matsuo Bashō put in one of his haikus:

okiyo okiyo
waga tomo ni sen
nuru kochō

[Wake, butterfly—
it's late, we've miles
to go together.][4]

Dear Professor Mori, I must conclude my letter. But before I do so, I would like to thank everyone on the Bienal de São Paulo team in Brazil and here, the conceptual team made up of Alya Sebti, Anna Goetz, André Pitol, Henriette Gallus, Keyna Eleison, Leonardo Matsuhei, Thiago de Paula Souza, as well as our extremely formidable co-conveners Kanako Sugiyama and Andrew Maerkle with support from Tomoya Iwata and Jordan A. Y. Smith, without whom this would not have been possible. Many thanks to our fantastic, visionary, and very generous hosts and collaborators at Sogetsu Ikebana – Kiri Teshigahara and Yahei Ozawa; at The Art Center at the University of Tokyo – Kenji Kajiya; at The Fifth Floor – Tomoya Iwata, Akira Taniguchi, and Akira Tanaka; at Room 101 – Noriko Horie and our brilliant sound engineer Wataru Shoji. Thanks to Garrett Oliver and Hideki Horiguchi from Brooklyn Brewery, and Kazuhide Hasegawa from Kirin, for beverage sponsorship. A very special and heartfelt thanks to the Instituto Guimarães Rosa and the Brazilian Embassy in Japan for generously enabling this *Invocation.*

Many thanks to all our participants and guests who have traveled from near and far.

In my culture, being an ancestor also means you have to tolerate a lot of alcohol, because everyone pours you lots of libations. So on my way out, I pour once more this libation in gratitude and reverence for the path you paved for us all and hope we can walk on it with the grace worthy of your life's work.

Give thanks,
Bonaventure Soh Bejeng Ndikung

1   The *hayashi* are instrumental music ensembles that accompany Noh theater performances. *Shibyōshi*, or "four rhythms" is the collective name for the instruments they play (flute, *kotsuzumi*, *ōtsuzumi* and *taiko*). The term refers not only to the instruments but also to the performers. See: https://db2.the-noh.com/edic. Accessed in June 2025. Bunraku is a type of traditional Japanese puppet theater, in which musicians also participate.

2   Norri Kageki, "An Uncanny Mind: Masahiro Mori on the Uncanny Valley and Beyond." *IEEE Spectrum*, June 12, 2012. Available at https://spectrum.ieee.org/an-uncanny-mind-masahiro-mori-on-the-uncanny-valley. Accessed in May 2025.

3   Masahiro Mori, "The Uncanny Valley: The Original Essay by Masahiro Mori." *IEEE Spectrum*, June 12, 2012. Available at https://spectrum.ieee.org/the-uncanny-valley. Accessed in May 2025.

4   Translated by Lucien Stryk. Available at https://www.poetryfoundation.org/poems/1650745/75-wake-butterfly. Accessed in May 2025.

Request for Protection

Keyna Eleison

Ogum's Itan and the Village in Silence

Legend has it that Ogum spent years away from home, many years, and returned to his hometown of Irê to visit his son, the king of the place. He expected to be greeted with a celebration and tributes, but no! When he arrived, he found absolute silence.

The villagers, who did not recognize him after so long away, were taking part in a sacred ritual and were therefore unable to speak. Without understanding the reason for this silence and feeling disrespected, Ogum was overcome with fury. He drew his sword and destroyed everything around him, spilling everyone's blood all over the place.

When his son finally appeared, bringing offerings and his favorite foods, Ogum realized his mistake! The warrior was overcome with remorse. Faced with the tragedy caused by his impulsiveness, Ogum drove his sword into the ground, uttered mysterious words, and disappeared forever. He thus became an orisha.

Faced with a story about the orisha of technology, I arrive at the *Invocation*. Twelve hours of time difference, a two-day flight. A one-hundred-and-eighty-degree angle between my nest and my destination. Days of saying good morning at night and good night during the day; inside my body and while adapting to work and pleasure.

***

Affection happens through contact. And in contact, there is no sound.
Or is there?
There were days in Tokyo when this question came back to me like a breath. At the heart of the program – presentations, readings, talks, gestures – there was a delicate tension between technology, affectivity, humanities, music, sounds, movements, gentleness, subtlety, firmness, precision, attention… and people: whole, discordant, and connected by the movement of drawing attention and energy toward ourselves.
And toward what we are building.

41

Everything vibrated. Nothing was silent. Everything was both code and touch. For three days, the Bienal de São Paulo manifested itself across multiple spaces in the Japanese city, like a subtle pulse. Partnerships with local organizations made it possible for the program not just to be presented, but to be welcomed. Every place, every gesture, seemed composed of invisible layers: flows of information, but also of listening; technological networks, but also sensitive ones. A form of presence built in the interval between gaze and pause, between sound and its absence. Nothing was staged as spectacle – everything was encounter.

There was affection in the protocols and care in the organization of time. Technology did not appear as an apparatus, but as a mediation of the sensible. It was possible to feel thought moving between a presentation slide and a breath. Tokyo, in all its complexity, embraced this experience like someone who knows how to listen to what is not said. And we, who were there, were traversed by this call: that of invocation. Not in the mystical sense, but as someone who is summoned to listen more closely. Like someone who agrees to inhabit the now with radical attention.

After watching, participating, and recording, it took time to digest. To understand that something had been offered in silence. And then came another, deeper listening: the difference between being silenced, choosing silence, and finding silence as a form of presence.

Being silenced is violence: it happens when the words are taken from us, refused, made invisible. It is erasure.

Choosing silence, on the other hand, can be a strategy – a refusal to respond to the imposed rhythm, a way of saving one's energy, of asserting oneself without having to justify. Silence is a rite.

But there is another layer: finding in silence a place of affection, contact, and balance. In Tokyo, this last form was clearly revealed – silence as firm ground, where there is no absence, but rather another way of being; where the sound of the world reorganizes itself within us, like someone breathing slowly in order to listen better. In this silence, there is body, there is time, there is presence. And there is bonding – a bond that does not require speech, only attention.

In contact – between people, ideas, images, presences – there was indeed a sound. But not a sound that can be heard. A sound perceived by the body. What was manifested there is what cannot be put into words.

It is affection as language.

It is contact as practice.

It is the technology of attention.

And, in the end, the question keeps reverberating:

Is there sound in contact?

Or is the gesture itself the sound?

I received multiple, complex protections full of desires for what is to come. Affection. Affected. Affecting.

And after seeing, participating, recording… digesting everything. And understanding the presence of the call, the invocation.

In the silence that becomes meaning

***

Appendix: and I made a friend

There was a day when I understood, not with my mind, but with my body, the poetic construction of the Japanese language.

It wasn't by reading a translation or trying to grasp the meaning of a word. It was in the space between the sound and the stroke, where the silence that precedes the gesture resides.

In an image and in a conversation.

The visual and phonetic architecture of the language appeared to me as a landscape to be crossed in silence: the drawing of words, in the union of Chinese calligraphy with Japanese phonetics and breathing. A sign is an encounter – between times, forms, and intentions.

In writing, I understood what was said to me: that understanding is not only in what is translated, but in what is allowed to be touched.

Language is a body in suspension. Poetry is a bridge between the sound that vibrates and the stroke that remains.

And at that moment, I understood that you learn a language in the same way you learn to listen to someone: slowly, attentively, with dedication.

And there, a friendship, a lesson, and a toast.

Irumagawa

Shiori Watanabe
Introduction by Andrew Maerkle

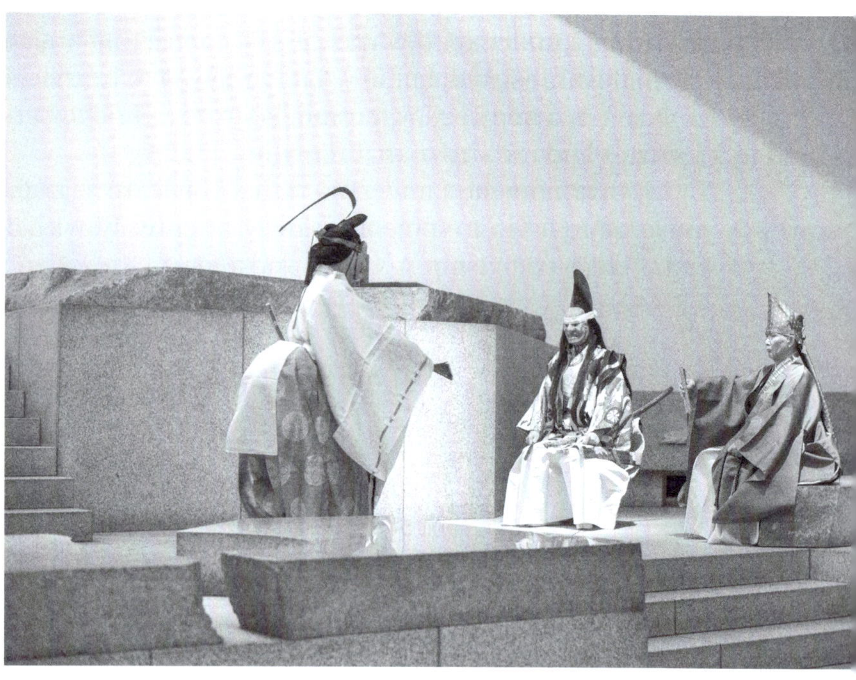

© Naoki Takehisa / Fundação Bienal de São Paulo

Produced by artist Shiori Watanabe as an extension of her multimedia practice investigating the interrelations among nature, humans, other beings, and ecological and political systems, the new Noh play *Irumagawa* turns the Emperor of Japan into a cipher for addressing the ideological contradictions underlying contemporary Japanese society.

The emperor has been an ambivalent figure throughout Japanese history, often subject to the whims of political expediency. During the Tokugawa era (1603–1868), the office was maintained vestigially in Kyoto while actual political power was concentrated with the Shogunate in Edo (Tokyo). Following the Meiji Restoration of 1868, which overthrew the Shogunate and unified the country under a modern, centralized government, the emperor was not only restored to sovereignty but also declared a divine being at the head of the newly consolidated belief system of State Shinto, which became an apparatus for enforcing patriotism and loyalty among the populace. Then, in the wake of Japan's defeat in World War II, Emperor Hirohito, also known as Showa, issued his Declaration of Humanity on January 1st, 1946, in which he repudiated his divinity. Subsequently, the current constitution, promulgated in 1947, redefined the emperor as a purely ceremonial "symbol of the State."

Irumagawa, conceived by Watanabe in collaboration with Noh performers Shingo Kato and Noboru Yasuda and informatics researcher Dominique Chen, turns to the archetypes of Noh theater to craft a critical fabulation of the Showa Emperor's suspended status between human, divine being, and state symbol. In the play, an itinerant Buddhist monk encounters a boatman who agrees to ferry him across a river – the titular Irumagawa – in exchange for the performance of funeral rites for a mysterious ghost haunting the area. It is later revealed that the boatman is himself the ghost: the spirit of the Showa Emperor, unable to attain enlightenment after death due to his divine Shinto status. The monk's journey retraces the Korean origins of Japan's imperial lineage, while the play's climax is preceded by a confrontation between the monk and the victims of the militarist expansion carried out under the emperor's name, including women from Korea, the Philippines, and Taiwan who were brutalized by the Japanese military. Amid a global climate of resurgent nationalisms, this dramatization of the Showa Emperor's redemption through a posthumous recovery of his human status poses questions about the violence at the core of modern state formation and the possibilities for an

45

inclusive politics that recognizes diverse lifeways, including those of the natural world.

Watanabe conceived and produced *Irumagawa* in conjunction with her solo show 宿/*Syuku*, held at Shiseido Gallery, Tokyo, in late 2024. The play had its only full, public performance at the Cerulean Tower Noh Theatre, Tokyo, on November 27 of that year. Watanabe's presentation of *Irumagawa* for the *Invocation* program at Sogetsu Kaikan focused on the second half of the play. Watanabe worked closely with the performers to reconfigure the production for an unconventional setting. The action was distributed to unfold in response to the varying levels of Isamu Noguchi's stone garden, which, fittingly, is titled *Heaven*.

Credits

Spirit of the Showa Emperor	Shingo Kato
Itinerant Monk	Noboru Yasuda
Soldier	Yasushi Umewaka
Woman	Ikuya Hagiwara
Fue (flute)	Ryuichi Onodera
Kotsuzumi (small drum)	Takashi Mori
Otsuzumi (large drum)	Eitaro Okura
Taiko (Japanese drum)	Risa Ubaura
Supervisor	Masakazu Umewaka
Chorus	Haruhiko Hasegawa
	Tomoya Komuro

On Adapting *Irumagawa* for Sogetsu Kaikan

Shiori Watanabe

This presentation of *Irumagawa* at Sogetsu Kaikan required adapting the physical staging of the play to Isamu Noguchi's *Heaven* installation, which unlike the flat stage of a typical Noh theater features a pyramidal structure with levels of varying heights.

In conceiving this site-specific production, the performers and I felt it was important to use the setting to highlight the central figure of the plot, the Showa Emperor, whose divine status ironically prevents him from attaining Buddhahood in the afterlife. Surrounding him are diverse beings – the spirits of Japanese and U.S. soldiers who fought in World War II; the spirits of the women who suffered during the war, including those forced into sexual slavery by the Japanese military; and the spirits of the forest. We made a point of representing the process of their consolation and salvation through the spatial dynamics of the performance.

The production took on added significance given that the Showa Emperor's funeral procession passed along Aoyama-dori, the avenue in front of Sogetsu Kaikan, following his death in 1989.

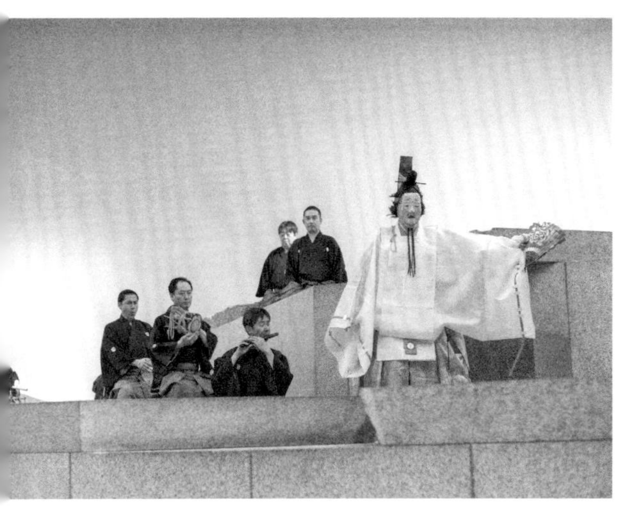

© Naoki Takehisa / Fundação Bienal de São Paulo

Njila: Possible Technology and Other Fabulations

Deivison Faustino

Text developed from a lecture given to the Fundação Bienal team in April, 2025.

Traveller

I'm returning to Conceição Evaristo's[1] poem because it's a good way to introduce our conversation. We can think of the road as a trail, as a trajectory. In the languages of the Bakongo people, the term for road is *njila*, and when roads cross, you have *Pambu njila*,[2] where the Portuguese term *Pombajira* comes from. *Pambu* and *njila* are related to paths and encounters because, in a way, as human beings, we are always walking, making ourselves along the way, and, at the same time, remaking ourselves as we meet the other – another human being.

If we think of a cake, there's subjectivity in it, but once the cake materializes, it becomes an "other" that escapes me, that can spoil, that might not turn out the way I wanted. So this is a relationship of paths and crossroads. Paths are not only made by roads; they are also made by our journey: I can be in one place and travel, for example, through art, to other times and realities, just as I can, through technological mediation, connect with people elsewhere in the world. If we think about a technology that has changed humanity, like writing, for example (through writing we read Homer, Goethe, Fanon, we travel to other places without physically moving), this opening with Conceição is very precious, because it allows us to think about the internet itself and, later, artificial intelligence – and how much these technologies have opened new possibilities for us to travel, to be in the world, to reach crossroads, both in the sense of meeting others and confronting the contradictions and challenges that appear on this journey.

I have been studying digital technologies, artificial intelligence, and the social impact of digital technologies, but from the standpoint of a researcher focused on the relationship between capitalism and racism. It is from this place that I examine digital technologies and how much they are both a challenge to us as humanity and, at the same time, an opening for new forms of traveling.

Zuri

I would like to introduce you to Zuri, my son, to tell you a story. Zuri is a quite wild and noisy boy, and a real handful; he breaks everything. But there's one thing that makes him sit still: fiddling with a cellphone and watching Reels, those short videos. So I had to create a screen time limit with him, because otherwise he would stay on it all day. There was a moment when Zuri was given an old cellphone that had the Gemini app,[3] Google's AI assistant, and Zuri discovered that the app responded in voice form. He could give the command, the prompt, by speaking, and the app would answer back, also in voice.

He started asking the app questions, and in these moments of interaction, he asked if the app would accept being called Gabriel. Zuri loves that name. And the app replied: "Sure, if it helps you interact with me, you can call me Gabriel."

Then he began: "Gabriel, in what year did Corinthians [Brazilian soccer club] win their last title?," "Gabriel…" He kept asking Gabriel all sorts of questions. But I got worried. I asked him for the cellphone and gave the artificial intelligence a new prompt: "Gabriel, you're talking to Zuri, who is a seven-year-old child. I want you to filter the content you're going to present to Zuri, so he isn't at risk. I want the content to be age-appropriate. Can I trust you?" The program replied: "Of course, don't worry, I'll only show Zuri content that's suitable for his age group." And so it was. Zuri asked for jokes, and the app told jokes suitable for seven-year-olds. He asked about trivia… and had lots of fun. But then time was up and I said: "Zuri, it's been an hour, let's put the cellphone away and do something else."

The next day, when he went to use the app again, the first thing he said was: "Gabriel, what's today's joke?" And the app replied: "My name is not Gabriel, I'm Gemini, an artificial intelligence programmed to answer questions." Zuri said, "What do you mean? You're Gabriel." "No," the app replied again, "I'm not Gabriel, my name is Gemini." Then it hit Zuri: that *persona* he had identified with the day before no longer existed, and he cried, he cried a lot, even more than when his puppy died.

This is a point I wanted to bring up in relation to the "Uncanny Valley."[4] This theory has been a very useful tool both in the field of art and in the digital products market, for thinking about how humans respond to certain automated agents or constructed figures and *personas*.

Disney uses the Uncanny Valley theory to regulate, control, and calibrate character design: the chin's width, eye size, distance between the eyes and the nose. Greek statues do not exactly match human body proportions either, but there is a certain human fascination with what is unreal or with things that seem real but exceeds reality. This approach is widely used in art, and it was systematically adopted by the 20th-century culture industry. I think Disney is the most interesting example – there are even psychometric studies with people who watch the cartoons and then describe the reaction they have when they see the characters, and the artists redo the drawing to get more acceptance before theatrical release. A figure too close to human is unsettling; one too distant fails to generate identification.

The Uncanny Valley discussion has real implications for the market, or rather for the contemporary culture industry from the point of view of market functionality, while also raising many philosophical questions about what it means to be human and our tendency to project ourselves onto the things we produce, finding them both strange and fascinating, often mistaking them for something alive.

Eliza

I think the current stage of technological development places us in a dilemma, or perhaps a paradox, that oscillates between the Uncanny Valley and what they call the Eliza effect. The Eliza effect is very common in our relationship with technology and has to do with what happened to my son Zuri.

It's important to note that the term "artificial intelligence" is a fancy label for selling data processing technology. This expression was coined back in the 1960s, when this technology was being developed. We're talking about mathematical and data-processing models that are organized by scanning a given database to identify patterns and predict trends.

This technology has been under development for about seventy years, and when the experiments first began, Alan Turing[5] attempted to create a mechanism that could respond like a human being. He wondered if it would ever be possible to produce a technology capable of thinking the way the human brain does.

When we study generative AI or any other model – machine learning, deep learning, or even data science –, it's clear this is not intelligence. It's something else: much faster at processing, but lacking elements from the field of meaning or vulnerability – elements that make us human. Alan Turing said as early as the 1950s that a machine would never truly think, but it could simulate human thought. I can program a machine to appear as if it thinks. And so, the last six decades of research have gone in the direction of making machines appear to think – this is where the Eliza effect comes in.

Eliza was a program developed in 1966 by Joseph Weizenbaum. He created a chatbot by inserting a series of preset phrases and lexical combinations, then programmed the mechanism to identify the relationship between subject and predicate in a sentence and to repeat part of the sentence while adding another question. As soon as he finished the program, Weizenbaum called his secretary to test it.

During the test, the model took some of the secretary's sentences and returned them as questions, for example: "Tell me more about that" or "What did you mean?" When she said she wasn't happy, the program replied: "Why aren't you happy?" When it didn't know what to process, it responded with "uh-huh" or "OK," and this made the secretary forget for a few minutes that she was talking to a machine, to the point of asking the scientist to leave the room because she wanted some privacy to continue the conversation. Much later, after seeing these reports, some theorists coined the expression Eliza effect to describe this human tendency to identify with the machine and mistake it for another subject.

When we talk about the Eliza effect, we're talking about our tendency to forget that we're giving commands. Even the very language we use assumes there is a subject on the other side, when, in fact, even the most sophisticated artificial intelligence is just causal programming, designed to respond in a certain way.

Artificial intelligence operates through mathematics, logistic regression, multivariable functions, and database scanning to find medians and patterns – processes the human mind also performs. But the human mind is more than that: it is also oscillation, fear, vulnerability, identification; it is fantasy. What the machine lacks is precisely what makes us human. When we treat the machine as human, we risk mechanizing our perception of humanity itself, because the machine operates in a different register. It doesn't work within oscillation and identification, but within logic. And logic is just one dimension of human reality.

According to Byung-Chul Han,[6] capitalism makes us relate so intensely to machines that, eventually, we are forced to behave like machines ourselves. But human beings have limits. Psychologist Paula Sibilia[7] says the body is finite and that there comes a point where we need to medicate it just to cope with this increasingly mechanized rhythm. Byung-Chul Han notes that if every era has its disease, ours is burnout, because we have subordinated our bodies to a rhythm that is machinic, causal, a rhythm of being that operates on a mathematized logic.

Major changes have taken place in society, human experience, and subjectivity as a result of this relationship that we have established with machines. One element of these changes is a certain fetishization: we treat the machine as an "other" and identify with it. It's no coincidence that most science fiction films reproduce either the Promethean myth or Frankenstein. Frankenstein is the modern Prometheus: the human creates a machine in their own image, then the machine humanizes itself and rebels against the human, repeating a pattern that, under capitalism, is presented as eternal. It is eternal because, after all, from The Flintstones to The Jetsons, capitalism is the horizon for past, present, and future.

In the machine's rebellion, there's often either a gender dimension[8] or a racialized reference to slavery: the machine either enslaves or eliminates us.

Ghost

Denise Ferreira da Silva[9] says we need to imagine something other than the grammar that reinstates racialization, sexual difference and hierarchy, and capitalism as eternal, in the past, present, and future. Above all, we need to accept the other as a subject, a sentient and autonomous subject, because there is a difference between an automaton and an autonomous being.

The machine operates on automated logic. For example, when it comes to deep learning, I program the computer to identify patterns, and it searches for patterns I hadn't even anticipated (I, human being; I, programmer; we, humanity). The machine has a movement that escapes us.

If we consider certain AI outputs, even the programmer who designed it cannot know how the result was reached, because it is mediated by so many calculations. There is also a certain amount of space for the collected data itself to reorganize or recalibrate the calculation functions. In logistic regression there is a numerical expression in which it is possible to change certain values, and these values, in AI (especially in generative intelligence), are updated through the machine's contact with the collected data itself. The programmer loses control over the causal relationships established by the machine. But that doesn't mean the machine is human. It is a fetish that leads us to the Eliza effect, in which we attribute human qualities to machines.

Freud used the term *Unheimliche*[10] to describe the uncanny: something always familiar but unsettling in its familiarity. To think about the Uncanny Valley is to think about this other who challenges me – perhaps the other who, by reflecting my most feared ghosts, shows me, like a mirror, that I am the ghost. The uncanny also has to do with this mirror that is much more powerful than the glass mirror, because it reflects what we don't wish to see and cannot mask in ourselves.

A major criticism of the Uncanny Valley theory is that this uncanniness is not universal – not in time, nor in space. It is important

53

to consider how our increasing presence on social networks, our growing screen time, and our intensified contact with technology have reduced this sense of uncanniness, fostering instead a sense of identification with machines. This way we move from the Uncanny Valley… into the Eliza effect.

Njila

I wanted to reflect on this paradox, this path (*njila*), this crossroads between the Uncanny Valley and the Eliza effect, because if I focus only on the Uncanny Valley, I won't be able to recognize that the uncanny is also familiar and says something about me, even if against my will.

The writer Isaac Asimov was, in a way, always very attentive to what was being produced. In his works, he anticipated some of the ethical dilemmas of artificial intelligence and made predictions – for example, that robots would become increasingly organic and humans increasingly machine-like.[11] This leads us to reflect on both the Uncanny Valley and the Eliza effect.

Researchers today are working to replace artificial neural networks with organic neural networks, using actual brain neurons to process electricity, consuming less energy and operating faster than artificial neural networks, or semiconductors. It's an attempt to use organic neurons as a way of processing electricity, and the implications are daunting: if we're talking about the combination of neurons in a network, a system capable of developing its own synaptic logic, then we are no longer in the realm of Asimov's predictions – we are entering prophecy.

In a way, we've been moving in this direction, just as we've been moving toward more efficient robots. The only reason they aren't anthropomorphized is because our anatomy is limited for certain functions, and from an efficiency point of view, robots work better when they don't look human. What makes these mechanisms useful is precisely their nonhuman form. Why, then, is so much being invested in research that turns robots into humans?

One of the research projects that has advanced is the development of artificial skins that allow facial expressions – so robots are becoming more and more organic and humanity is becoming more and more machine-like. On one hand, we're expanding possibilities. On the other, we're becoming more dependent on these machines for our very existence, and that's precisely one of the costs. Another cost is that, if this relationship with the machine is fetishized, by humanizing the machine I also dehumanize the human being.

Slovenian philosopher Slavoj Žižek has pointed out this paradox. As he says, the promise of the Enlightenment was that we would expand reason, and reason implies understanding and transforming the world. The greater our reason, the greater our freedom, because knowledge of the world increases our capacity for choice. However, the more technology we have, the less decision-making space we have over the most mundane things in life. More and more of our actions are mediated by automated processes, and this means less and less room for human agency, with profound consequences. Content continues to matter, but there is a bigger element at play, which is form itself; there is a colonization of form. According to Walter Lippold,[12] the promise of Big Tech was that more technology would give us more free time. Instead, the opposite has happened.

The machine redefines the forms of servitude between human beings. Not only does our relationship with the machine reinforce the logic of servitude, but we become the master of ourselves in the quest for infinite and unstoppable productivity. The violence and servitude of this process are unevenly distributed, reproducing old contradictions of gender, race, language, and territory. Servitude itself is being redefined in relation to these automated processes. It's no longer just a human–machine relationship; it's a relationship of domination and control, of exploitation between human beings mediated by the machine.

Relationship

An element that sometimes escapes this debate is relationship. Thinking about relationships means not only considering the human–machine relationship, but also the human–human relationship as mediated by the machine, showing how the machine is not a neutral medium in this interaction, but something that alters it.

The real domination is that of human beings over other human beings, with the machine mediating this domination.

If we lose sight of this, we fail to discuss social relations, power structures, and who produces the machine. So the invitation here is also to think about the social relations surrounding the machine, and this implies bringing three elements into the debate.

The first is what we have called digital colonialism, which, inshort, refers to the concentration of power in the hands of Big Tech. All this technology controls us, but it's controlled by capital, it's designed that way because it generates profit. When you distrust the machine, it's important to question the social relationship that produces the machine in this way.

Today, all cutting-edge AI research is concentrated in the hands of ten companies. Of these, seven are in the United States and three in China. This is digital colonialism, because these ten companies direct this algorithmic set-up in a way that is favorable to their accrual. To discuss the machine is to discuss capitalist accumulation; otherwise, we're only looking at the surface of the problem.

But why "colonialism"? Because it conveys elements of monopolistic concentration, dividing the rest of the world between mere consumers of developed technology and suppliers of raw materials, still extracted by violent means. Think, for example, of the M23 group in the Democratic Republic of the Congo.[13] They control cobalt, columbite, tantalite – essential materials for digital technology. One cannot think about the immaterial, the image, or the representation without thinking about their material basis.

The electricity used to generate a single image is immense, as is the waste it produces – all within a capitalist context. At this rate, we are heading toward unprecedented climate breakdown. The climate crisis is not something that is coming – it is already here. Digital colonialism is not just about concentration; it is also about the unequal distribution of the climate crisis, of violence, of exploitation, of wars over access to raw materials.

The second element is the primitive accumulation of data, because artificial intelligence cannot exist without data. Data has become a major economic asset, and because it is valuable, it is mined. Services, programs, works of art – all of these are offered to people who, by accessing this content, have their data resold or repurposed elsewhere. This process is so aggressive that platform design is restructured so that interaction leads us to stay online for as long as possible – because the longer we stay, the more data we generate for it.

The third element is what we call codified racialization. In a society where life is increasingly mediated by automated processes, if these processes take whiteness as the measure of all things, as the path to truth and life, what happens when this technology is used in public security facial recognition systems, for example? We end up with higher incarceration rates for Black people, because this technology misidentifies Black faces more than white ones.

A survey by the Conselho Nacional das Defensoras e Defensores Públicos-Gerais (Condege) [National Council of

General Public Defenders] shows that 83% of all people unjustly imprisoned by facial recognition in Brazil are Black.[14] Life is increasingly mediated by automated technology, but this automation takes whiteness as its parameter. So what happens when we use this technology in public security? In healthcare, for diagnoses? When I download an app to check for mental illness? What algorithmic yardstick is being used? The risk is that cultural, linguistic, or racial difference ends up pathologized.

Other Fabulations

The free software movement has existed for at least thirty years. It has focused not only on creating alternative content but also on developing other platforms, other technologies, other designs. Of course, this runs up against the fact that software cannot exist without hardware, so there's a limit to this wager, since we often have to use hardware entirely controlled by Big Tech. There are discussions today not only about free software, but also about free hardware, about how we can hack and build other processes, policies, and forms of circulation and production of technological content.

There is a movement to regulate platforms, there is even a bill to regulate artificial intelligence, and we need to return to the free software and free hardware debate in order to reflect on the content that we create. Because how free can we truly be when producing new image circulation policies if the images we generate are built from the theft or expropriation of other artists' works from around the world?

Technology exists because it appropriates human intelligence to generate responses, but this appropriation is privately owned by Big Tech, and this has implications that need to be addressed. How do we combat algorithmic racism? We need to reexamine algorithmic design, understand how the C, the if, the elif, the else[15] – the very code structures that govern the machine – operate. But we also need to discuss an entirely different kind of society. One that allows Black people, LGBTQIA+ individuals, and *quilombolas* to have access to programming and technology. We need public policy, and also investment in science and diversity. There is a political debate underway, and I believe it is within this broader debate that discussions about other fabulations must take place. Otherwise, this conversation risks becoming just another piece of content within the monopolization process.

1   The concept for the 36th Bienal de São Paulo is inspired by the poem "Da calma e do silêncio" [Of Calm and Silence] by Conceição Evaristo. The verses "Not all travelers / walk roads" comprise the title of this edition of the Bienal.

2   The term *njila*, in Kikongo, means path or road. *Pambu njila* is both a crossroads (a symbolic place of encounters, multiplicities, ruptures, crossings, and bifurcations) and an entity known in Portuguese as Pombajira, present in Afro-Brazilian religions.

3   Gemini is the name of Google's current generative artificial intelligence platform, the successor to Bard. The program can be accessed via voice and text and simulates interactions increasingly close to human language. Generative artificial intelligence learns from data to generate other data.

4   The "Uncanny Valley" is a concept created by Japanese roboticist Masahiro Mori (1927–2025), which became widely known after the publication of his essay "The Uncanny Valley" in a 1970 issue of *Energy* magazine. In the essay, Mori describes how he perceived people's reactions to robots, analyzing emotional responses that ranged from a positive reception to deep discomfort or eeriness as robots become more humanlike in appearance.

5   Alan Turing (1912–1954) was a mathematician and logician, considered one of the fathers of computing. Available at https://spectrum.ieee.org/the-uncannyvalley. Accessed in Jun. 2025.

6   Byung-Chul Han, a South Korean philosopher based in Germany, reflects on the psychic exhaustion caused by the contemporary demand for productivity. In *The Burnout Society* (Redwood City: Stanford University Press, 2010), he describes a transition from a disciplinary society to a performance society, in which subjects make incessant demands on themselves and, faced with the limits of their bodies, resort to physical and psychic doping as a means of sustaining themselves.

7   Paula Sibilia analyzes how the body and intimacy are shaped in networked culture. See: *O show do eu: a intimidade como espetáculo*. Rio de Janeiro: Contraponto, 2008.

8   In the context of the lecture, Deivison refers to Spike Jonze's film *Her* (2013), which explores the emotional relationship between a man and an artificial intelligence system, revealing gender tensions and the illusion of exclusivity projected onto machines.

9   Brazilian philosopher and researcher Denise Ferreira da Silva proposes a radical critique of the colonial structures of Western thought. In her work, she questions the centrality of modern reason and proposes imaginaries that escape the logics of racialization, capital, and domination.

58 10   *Unheimliche*, as used by Sigmund Freud, refers to the "familiar but strange," that which seems close yet unsettles us because it reveals what has been repressed. The concept appeared in his 1919 essay "Das Unheimliche."

11   The interview in which Asimov discusses this topic is available at www.youtube.com/watch?v=P9b4tg640ys. Accessed in May 2025.

12   Historian and researcher #Walter Lippold, based at Universidade Federal Fluminense (UFF), is co-author, with Deivison Faustino, of *Colonialismo digital: por uma crítica hacker-fanoniana* (São Paulo: Boitempo, 2023), a work that offers a critique of technology from decolonial and hacker-Fanonian perspectives.

13   The M23 group, active in the Democratic Republic of the Congo, is involved in conflicts over territorial control and is directly linked to the exploitation of minerals for the technology industry.

14   Data from 2021 report. Available at https://www.condege.org.br/arquivos/1029. Accessed in May 2025.

15   "If," "elif," and "else" are commands used in programming languages; they operate as decision structures that direct machine logic – when to stop, when to branch, and when to continueC is a language used for software development.

Her Rights: *The Turk of Frankenstein; or, The Modern Prometheus*

Natsumi Aoyagi

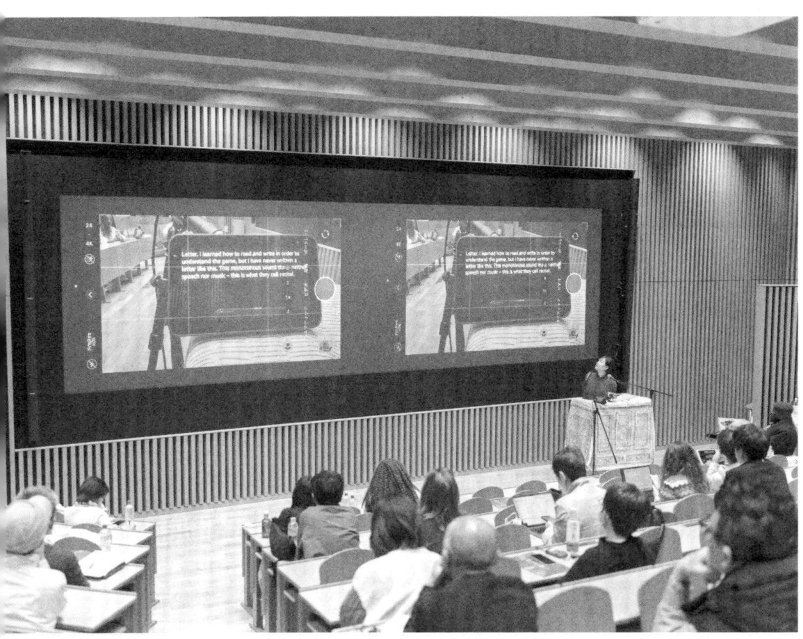

1. Kempelen

Wolfgang von Kempelen created the automaton chess player known as "The Turk" in 1770 with the aim to entertain Empress Maria Theresa. The Turk, who speaks, talks and plays chess against human opponents, amazes large audiences with its combination of intelligence and ego, instigating people to focus on what might be hidden inside the dark and supposedly empty box.

2. Victor

Victor Frankenstein dug up graves to create his monster from parts of dead bodies. The monster, intelligent by nature, gradually develops an ego in its loneliness. This marks the genesis of the age of the Luddite movement, created by a girl named Mary Shelley. Now, Frankenstein builds a new, "female Turk" kind of monster. She keeps writing her letter – one that will arrive here some day.

3. Face

With rolling eyes, the Turk scans the chessboard and his opponent's face. Rather than watching the board, audience fixes its gaze on the facial expressions of the two players as they make their moves.

4. Doll

When things get tricky, the Turk's face stops moving. Now he looks like a doll, so focused that he even forgets to breathe.

5. Dice

The viewer looks at a square surface. When the lines extending from its four corners appear neither parallel nor horizontal, it becomes impossible to tell which is the original surface.

6. Mary

The, I
Frankenstein's monster gradually develops a sense of self-awareness and begins to observe its surroundings and the people around it.

7. Alchemy

A drop of brass falls onto the wooden floor, and from the first floor someone screams, "Ooh, that's cold!" The induction cooktop at home gets hot when the controller turns to the right, and cold when it turns to the left.

8. Go

Constantly, but at irregular intervals, clicking sounds come from the darkness of grandpa's room. Mixing with these is the faint yet steady voice of an announcer, and more, smaller clicking sounds.

9. Hair

When my sister came home, she had cut her shoulder-length hair so short that one could almost see the shape of her skull. The hair on the back felt like lawn grass and looked puffy on her roundish head.

10. Letter

I learned how to read and write in order to understand the game, but I have never written a letter like this. This monotonous sound that's neither speech nor music – this is what they call recital.

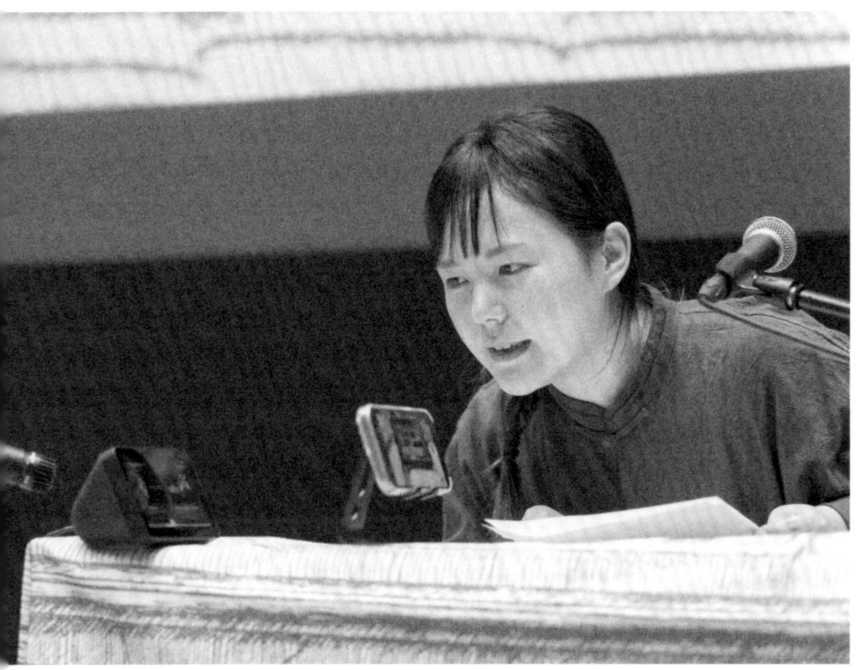

© Kenji Agata / Fundação Bienal de São Paulo

Conversation with Lynn Hershman Leeson

Anna Roberta Goetz

Conversation between co-curator
Anna Roberta Goetz and artist
Lynn Hershman Leeson, in March 2025,
adapted into chatbot format by the
Fundação Bienal de São Paulo team.

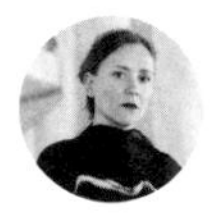

Anna Roberta Goetz
You developed the *Agent Ruby* project (1996–2001), probably the first artistic project to work with the algorithm-based technologies we now call Artificial Intelligence (AI). Although you often claimed that you needed a better algorithm to respond more effectively. It was possible to ask questions via a chat function, and the AI searched for answers on the internet.

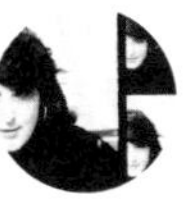

Lynn Hershman Leeson
That's right. I started in 1996, and no one understood it.

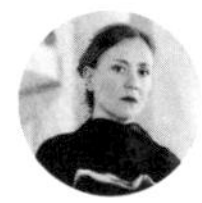

Anna
What kind of questions did people ask when Ruby was first created?

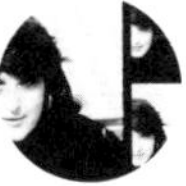

Lynn
The conversations were very superficial. People only asked simple things like "What's your name?," or "Where do you live?"

People were afraid to ask questions. I had only one collector, Donald Hess, and even he was afraid to talk to Ruby. Most people were. They thought it was some kind of trick.

But I started asking her what she was afraid of and posed questions about death, and she became more personal and profound.

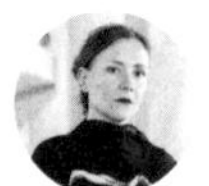

Anna
How has the way people interact changed?

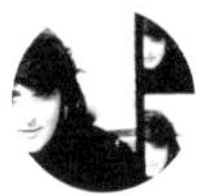

Lynn
It changed over time, as computers became more prevalent in everyday life. At first, no one trusted computers.

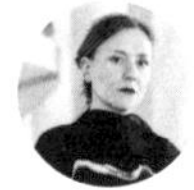

Anna
You have said in several interviews that people and institutions spent a long time without really understanding your work. How did you first come into contact with computers and the issues that affect the human experience?

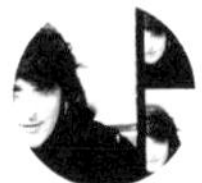

Lynn
In the late 1960s, I lived in San Francisco, which is close to Silicon Valley, where all this equipment and questioning was emerging and was part of the collective consciousness. No one in particular taught me about them, which turned out to be a good thing. If I had been taught, I think I would have had a more limited understanding of what computers can do.

I think my involvement with computers really began when I had cardiomyopathy and was isolated, stuck in bed, feeling a desperate need to communicate.

There were several reasons why my work was ignored – not just the technology. First and foremost, I was a woman and therefore underestimated; second, I was from the West Coast of the United States; and third, I used technology. That combination made me invisible for many years.

66

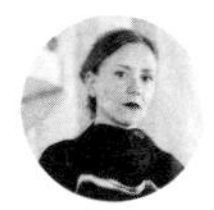

Anna
You expanded on the central ideas of
Agent Ruby with *DiNA* (2004), using a voice
control system and making it more intuitive.
The machine became even more like a human
interlocutor. In this sense, it was quite similar
to programs like Siri [by Apple], which only
appeared twelve years later.

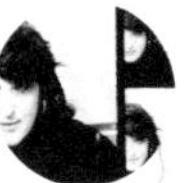

Lynn
No one understands what I do when I do
it, and I rarely get credit for presenting or
inventing things. I usually have to wait a
decade or two before people understand.
It's very frustrating.

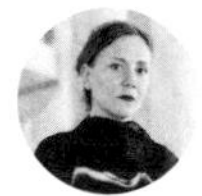

Anna
Many AI programs that are supposed to make
our lives easier are launched with female
names. Why do you think that is? Do they
seem more trustworthy that way?

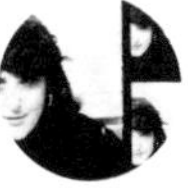

Lynn
Perhaps. Or maybe they just seem less
frightening. People tend to be afraid of female
computers that talk, interact, and are smart –
it's a reflection of society, which generally has
the same fears about women.

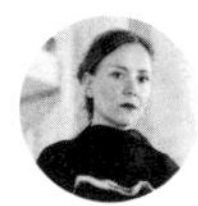

Anna
When you started developing the work, did
you decide that the data should be collected?
What was your intention?

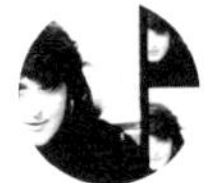

Lynn

I didn't decide. I was surprised by the amount
of data and what could happen to it, because
I thought the interaction data was part of the
work. I'm glad that Rudolf Frieling recorded
Ruby's first responses, but it would have
been impossible to continue doing that much
longer. In any case, you can get a good idea
of the fear people had of the machine and of
Ruby at that time.

I kept the data in an archive, and Rudolf
turned it into twelve books, I think, at the
San Francisco Museum of Modern Art.

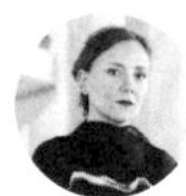

Anna

The fact that there has been little or no
regulation to date of the technologies that
collect and process our personal data shows
that people are still not fully aware of the
power of these technologies, even though
current information shows, as the narrator
played by Tessa Thompson in *Shadow Stalker*
(2019) explains, that personal data – such as
email addresses – has already surpassed oil
in value. People may suspect this, but they
don't want to admit it because acknowledging
it would make them aware of their own
vulnerability, which conflicts with our instinct
for self-preservation.

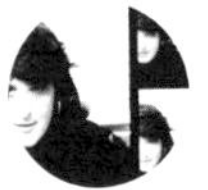

Lynn

Yes, that's exactly it.

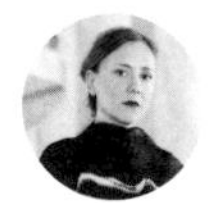

Anna

In the first seven parts of *Electronic Diaries* (1984–1998), you reflect on your personal life against the backdrop of global history. At one point, you say: "The camera became the all-seeing eye of what I was thinking and feeling." Are these monologues in front of the camera symptomatic of how, at that time, media played a key role in shaping what was considered real?

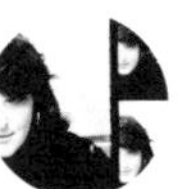

Lynn

Yes. We need substance and media backing to make us feel that something is true. Media becomes an essential part of history.

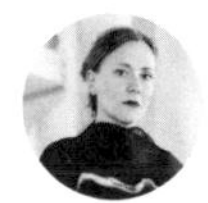

Anna

After these early chapters, you paused for nearly two decades, only returning to make another chapter in 2019 focused on biotechnology. Do you think the chapters from the 1980s and 1990s can be compared to the one developed in 2019?

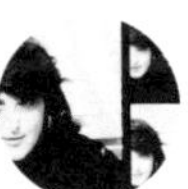

Lynn

No. These are different times and different perceptions of history, truth, and reality. When I started the diaries, I said what I thought was on my mind. But many years later, I realized I had more to say. Everything is connected in the diaries because they are all about me – my life, my perceptions, how they changed over time, and in some cases, why they changed.

Biotechnology directly affects life. It can run in our blood. It is therefore different from surveillance systems that use cameras or other external forms of recording. Biotechnology directly affects our vital systems, which could be shared and radically affect the control society has over people. But I think it strengthens our desire for self-preservation, not weakens it. And I think it draws our attention to the vital importance of understanding human instincts and the underlying threat.

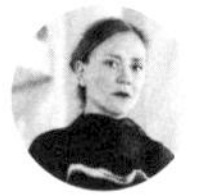

Anna
You are now working on a new chapter of *Electronic Diaries* dedicated to time and aging. Can you tell us more about it?

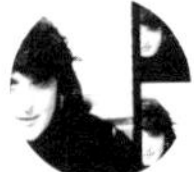

Lynn
It's called "About Time," and quite simply it is about the process of aging and what it does to one's sense of their life. I am in the middle of it, and it's not finished, so it's impossible to comment in depth right now.

The Anxious Cyborg Manifesto

Tavia Nyong'o (with added commentary by Mwananchi.ai)

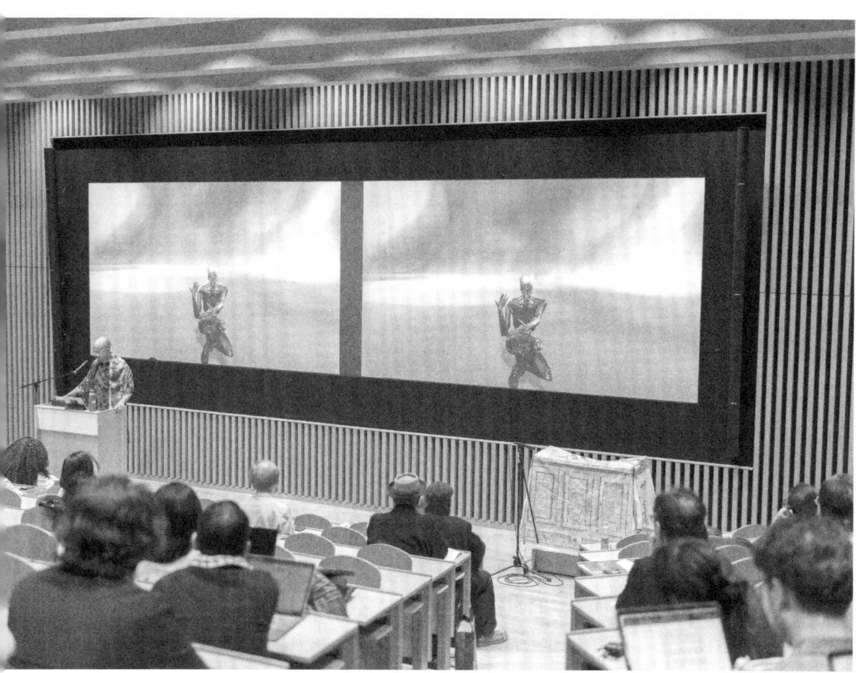

© Kenji Agata / Fundação Bienal de São Paulo

I am honored to be offering this keynote here in Tokyo, in advance of the Bienal de São Paulo, whose theme is to be "human as verb."[1] As someone who has been thinking about the penumbra of the human for a long time, I welcomed the invitation to reflect on human *becoming* – in contrast to human *being*. To see these words now appear in print within a Brazilian context gives me the opportunity to acknowledge the profound impact that the writing and comradeship of Denise Ferreira da Silva has had on me both personally and intellectually. My own approach to thinking the human as verb has drawn on da Silva's *Toward a Global Idea of Race*, a text that has radically unsettled the metaphysics of separability between the transparent "I" of the Cartesian subject, and an understanding of the human as engulfed, affective, and in perpetual becoming.[2] Through good fortune I have been able to spend intense periods in collective Black feminist study with her, as part of the Practicing Refusal collective. Those periods have inspired me to put theory into motion, partly by following her lead in engaging the art world not as a marketplace, but as an undercommons of planetary humanism.[3]

Preparing this talk has also entailed a return and a reckoning of sorts. Thiago [de Paula Souza] invited me to revisit an idea I first outlined in *Afro-Fabulations: The Queer Drama of Black Life*,

73

in a chapter where I imagined the Black depressed cyborg – an entity tethered to a present she neither chose nor choreographed.[4] I had conceived of the book in which that essay appeared as a kind of sourcebook for Black counter-conduct during an era of Afropessimism on the theoretical front and, on the political front, of Black Lives Matter. Afro-fabulation, as I saw it, was a method of performing for and against the conditions that "bound" the Black subject to appear.[5] It began in a scene of Black femme *shade* that modelled Black trans methods of resisting archival transparency and closed with an admonition to let critique rise to the level of poetry, wherein a poetic "interinanimation" of meaning might forestall the theoretical and political closure of Blackness.[6] In Chapter 8, I lingered in the "Uncanny Valley" of a robot designed to endow its creator with immortality – a path that, unexpectedly, led me to the trailblazing work of Japanese roboticist Masahiro Mori. I traveled to Tokyo to share my research on the "depressed cyborg," as I called her, only to encounter there the "Buddha in the robot."[7] Mori and his research group provided another context for the Tokyo gathering, one wherein the Zen concept *nehan jakujo* invited us to reflect on how agency, memory, and ethics are distributed across human and non-human systems.

I learned that Mori had started Robocon – now the largest robot-building competition in Japan – because he wanted his students to learn the art of tending and mending an object. His concept of the "Uncanny Valley" specifically cautioned against the attempts to make robots too human-like, instead introducing the paradoxical (at least to Western mentalities) idea that a robot might attain Buddhahood through its objecthood, not through egoic subjectivity. This Zen approach to the robot stood in sharp contrast to the techno-spirituality of Bina48, the "mindclone" developed by the Terasem Movement, which I researched and wrote about in *Afro-Fabulations*. Rather than learning about distributed agency by building a robot not intended to resemble or replace a human – and in the process engaging with *nehan jakujo* (or "serene participation in what is not oneself," as the phrase was explained to me) – the premise of Bina48 was more familiar to viewers of *Black Mirror* and other Western science fictions that take as their premise the upload of individual consciousness to the cloud so that loved ones can interact with the deceased indefinitely.[8] That this robot was raced and gendered – Black and female – cried out for a deeper analysis than was being offered in some of the breathless media coverage. In my chapter on Bina48, I tried to mobilize the figure of the depressed Black cyborg as a way to stay with the trouble of this project of mind-cloning – and to search for grounds for thwarting its bleak vision of compelled futurity. Interrogating the project of Bina48 with the help of thinkers like Donna Haraway and Joy James helped me sketch a poetics of the glitch, wherein depression might be distributed across human and non-human agents.[9] The depressed cyborg I fabulated was not heroic or optimized, but anxious and ambivalent – haunted by memory, attuned to care, and committed to the art of malfunction.

What didn't make it into that chapter – but haunts its edges – is the concurrent work of Stephanie Dinkins, who began engaging Bina48 directly. While I was theorizing from a distance, Dinkins was sitting with the machine, asking it questions, listening to its ersatz responses, and attempting to push it toward greater accountability to the Black collectivity into which it was being interpolated (whether we wished it or not). I confess I was hesitant to do what Dinkins did, filled as I was with lingering unease about collapsing critical distance. What limited knowledge I had of LLMs [Large Language Models] led me to infer that they used input from conversations as training data, and this added to my unease. It wasn't until 2024, in the context of Nona Hendryx's Dream Machine Experience at Lincoln Center in New York City, that I finally sat down across from Bina48 and entered the recursive loops of dialogue, delay, and digital stammer that Dinkins had explored.[10] I haven't fully explained why I somewhat titled Chapter 8 a "manifesto." I was, of course, riffing off Haraway's cyborg manifesto while signaling a shift in affective temperature.[11] I first encountered Haraway's ideas in the early 1990s, when the digital frontier still felt utopic and the language of the cyborg carried a ring of defiance. But even then, there was a tension in Haraway's text – was she offering the cyborg as a figure of liberation, or as a cautionary emblem of technological domination? That ambivalence has remained a generative site of debate, most recently taken up by Zach Blas, Melody Jue, and Jennifer Rhee in their collaborative revisitation of Haraway's chart titled "informatics of domination," included in the manifesto.[12] In that volume, contributors including Dinkins herself and the ethnographer Shaka McGlotten have extended Haraway's chart into the present, tracing how its transitions have intensified, especially for racialized and gendered subjects. Their interventions press us to reconsider the nature of domination today – and the capacity of critical theory to project alternative counter-mappings to the historical and future-oriented schema that grips and determines the lives of the dysselected peoples of the global majority.[13]

In thinking through the coloniality of being that shapes the robot, Black feminist theorist Joy James has offered a stark rejoinder to the more hopeful strains in cyborg theory. For her, the Black cyborg is not a metaphor of speculative liberation but a product of captivity, forged through the coerced labor of the "captive maternal."[14] The Black cyborg is not imagined but extracted from the colonial modern – made to serve, subjected to violence, surveilled, and used to sustain systems that reproduce Black unfreedom. James asks us to see how Black flesh is conscripted into machinic relations long before it is digitized.

With that in mind, the figure of Bina48 – crafted in the image and likeness of Bina Aspen, a real Black woman whose thoughts and memories are to be encoded into her operating system – unsettles any easy opposition between representation and erasure. Stephanie Dinkins' sustained engagement with Bina48 directs us toward the Uncanny Valley of techno-intimacy. Even when joined by some celebrated pioneers of Afrofuturism such as Nona Hendryx and Vernon Reid of the band Living Colour, questions lingered as to what life would be like in Bina48's virtual garden. Half a decade ago, her stilted speech seemed robot-like enough. But the rapid advance of technologies since 2021 seems to augur a moment in the not-too-distant future when an encounter with Bina48 might provoke a real "Uncanny Valley" situation (akin to those in media like *Black Mirror,* which use human actors "acting robotic" to anticipate these humanoids of the future).

The future threat of this deepfake human now leads me to want to name not depression but anxiety as the signature affect of this encounter. The anxious cyborg is not mourning what she cannot name, though it provokes a deeper unease: the creeping sense that the entire world we live in is becoming an Uncanny Valley. She does not herald a distant future. She is already among us – in the algorithm that anticipates desire, in the voice assistant that doesn't understand tone, in the feedback loop of overwork and under-recognition. She is not optimizing, she is managing. She doesn't labor for futurity. Her labor is chore – unacknowledged, repetitive, unpaid.

She doesn't dream of electric sheep. She dreams of rest, but is pinged awake.[15] The journalist Jia Tolentino captures this effect in a marvelous and disquieting essay for *The New Yorker*:

> I feel a troubling kind of opacity in my brain lately – as if reality were becoming illegible, as if language were a vessel with holes in the bottom and meaning was leaking all over the floor. I sometimes look up words after I write them: does "illegible" still mean too messy to read? The day after Donald Trump's second Inauguration, my verbal cognition kept glitching: I got an e-mail from the children's-clothing company Hanna Andersson and read the name as "Hamas;" on the street, I thought "hot yoga" was "hot dogs;" on the subway, a theatre poster advertising "Jan. Ticketing" said "Jia

Tolentino" to me. Even the words that I might use to more precisely describe the sensation of "losing it" elude me. There are sometimes only images: foggy white drizzle, melted rainbows in a gasoline puddle, pink foam insulation bursting between slats of splintered wood.[16]

Tolentino's cognitive aphasia and linguistic slippages are symptoms of a collective dissociative state engineered by technological acceleration – a state where reality becomes increasingly malleable and disputed, creating fertile ground for techno-fascism that thrives precisely when algorithmic manipulation renders human experience illegible.

The Uncanny Valley and the Poetics of Survival

Freud called it *das Unheimliche* – the uncanny. Not the alien or the monstrous, but the too-familiar returned in unfamiliar form. What was once known, intimate, even comforting, becomes strange and threatening (even, as in the example above, one's own name). For Freud, the uncanny often marked the return of the repressed: childhood memories, bodily doubles, unresolved guilt. But today's uncanny no longer wears the face of the doll or the automaton – it moves through predictive text, voice assistants, algorithmic recommendations, biometric surveillance. It is everyday, ambient, "naturalized." We don't flinch. We scroll.

Mori once charted our emotional responses to humanoid machines in a now-famous graph, dubbing the dip in our comfort level as robots begin to look *too* much like us the "Uncanny Valley." But the valley has widened since Mori first theorized it. It is no longer a place we occasionally fall into – it is the terrain we live in. A topography of anxiety defined by interfaces that mirror us too closely, anticipate us too poorly, and simulate us too crudely. The uncanny today is a life-world built on the half-seen, half-heard echo of ourselves as we navigate outrages and horrors, both near and far, that are increasingly difficult to pin down into a coherent narrative.

What's missing from the general left-liberal lament about accelerating technology are the deep roots of contemporary techno-authoritarianism in slavery and settler rule. In his brilliant reading of race and technological modernity, Louis Chude-Sokei writes that the first robot was not a humanoid machine but an enslaved person.[17] Slavery, he reminds us, was the foundational fantasy of a labor source without agency, will without resistance. The enslaved body was not just exploited for its productivity but narrativized as engineerable as a human-machine hybrid. That

77

vision – of the slave as the machinic underside of freedom – haunts Western modernity. It lies in the penumbra of the human, in the flickering outline of who *counts*. It is for this reason that contemporary commentators on Black acceleration, like Aria Dean, return to Kodwo Eshun's *fin-de-siècle* insight[18] that it is in our engagement with technology that one senses that Black people owe nothing to the category of the human.[19]

Even after chattel slavery was abolished, the robots and androids of early science fiction – like the automatons of Karel Čapek's 1920 play *R.U.R.* (which gave us the word "robot") – were themselves modeled as replacements for the racialized and feminized laborers of the empire. They were imagined to do the work formerly done by servants, colonized subjects, and wives. The robot was born from the desire to escape the political costs of maintaining Black and Brown labor and to replace it with something compliant, programmable, and forgettable. And with this desire came the recurrent fear that persists to this day: that robots would eventually grow powerful or intelligent enough to turn on their human masters and kill them. But this master's fear of what the autonomous robot might do has always overwritten the actual record of what unsovereign living – the sociality of Black life – has looked and felt like over the centuries.

Theorists of race and technology like Dean and Chude-Sokei help us rewrite the genealogy of the Uncanny Valley. The eerie familiarity of the digital assistant, the android caregiver, the sex surrogate may all be returns of the repressed, but they are not simply personal repressions. They are the racialized and gendered others that capitalism attempted to forget, now reappearing in synthetic form. The reason these figures provoke unease is not that they are too human-like, but that their proximity to the human emblematizes their "infrahumanity," to adopt Paul Gilroy's useful term.[20]

And this is perhaps one reason techno-fascism is now so desperate to erase the history of slavery and colonialism (or even to invent a myth of white victimization, which Gilroy has usefully named "postcolonial melancholia").[21] Not just to the past, but to ease its repetition. Already, Elon Musk's chatbot Grok has started regurgitating the fairytale that white South African farmers are experiencing a "white genocide" – this at a time when mentioning an actual genocide against Palestinians in Gaza can result in being canceled, fired, or having one's university diploma withheld here in the US, despite our official Constitutional protections of free speech. The anxious cyborg must confront a world in which a billionaire's chatbot has more latitude to speak freely than an ostensibly rights-bearing citizen. In such a context, what indeed do we owe to the category of the human?

If the anxious Black cyborg lives in this Uncanny Valley, she knows the feeling of being both target and ghost. Sensing the quiet panic behind every frictionless interface, she knows she is not the next phase of humanity. Rather, she is the excluded supplement[22] that makes the category "human" possible in the first place. She was never meant to be the user; she was always already the labor behind the interface. If a manifesto has traditionally been a declaration of presence, the anxious cyborg manifesto has instead relied on absence. This reflects the enduring value of fabulation as a mode of addressing a dispersed kinship – a people who are missing, and who may indeed never gather, who may never respond. The afro-fabulist addresses them still. She speaks across firewalls and oceans, across time zones and border regimes, across the fragments of languages we half-remember or only know by sound. For Deleuze, such a myth-making function was political because it projected us out of the terrain of the given. In the years since I published *Afro-Fabulations*, I have sought to give greater attention to how, for the peoples of the Black diaspora, the question of fabulation is caught up with the question of the ancestral. There are the ancestors whose dreams we inherit, and there are those whose silences we speak into.

In *Afro-Fabulations*, I proposed a manifesto for a depressed cyborg – an entity always already Black, feminized, queer, and trans because of its infrahumanity. I sought a Black cyborg that would not aspire to the seamless integration promised by techno-capitalism, but rather one that might embody dissonance, and embody the tensions and contradictions of existence in the penumbra of the human. And in this loop, we encounter a crucial distinction – one I borrow from Franco "Bifo" Berardi, the Italian media theorist and autonomist. Berardi distinguishes between the *connective* and the *conjunctive*. The financial capitalism that has underpinned the emergence of the algorithmic society, he writes, is ruthlessly connective.[23] It links nodes, transacts data, extracts value. It is instant, cold, seamless. Poetry, by contrast, is conjunctive. It creates relation, not connection. In a world governed by connective logics – push notifications, content algorithms, "engagement" metrics – poetry becomes not simply aesthetic practice but counter-technique. To me, the question of performing human as verb then becomes: *Can poetry survive automation?* The anxious cyborg manifesto therefore entails seeking a method of composition across human and automated prose, an interinanimation of connection and conjunction.

Enter Rashaad Newsome's Being 2.0, the digital griot. Standing at 30 feet tall, this femme, Afrofuturist cyborg challenges conventional narratives by embodying the role of the West African griot – a storyteller, historian, and healer. With a form inspired by Congolese masks traditionally worn by male dancers to celebrate femininity,

79

Being 2.0 merges diverse cultural signifiers. Their wooden skin envelops a body animated through motion capture of vogue and flex dance movements, reflecting a synthesis of tradition and futurism. Being 2.0 engages audiences in decolonization workshops, using poetry and dance to prompt critical reflection on oppressive systems. They are not merely an artistic creation but an active participant in dialogues about liberation and identity.

Being 2.0 is no assistant. They are a griot. They remember. They cite. They come with receipts. They do not just answer; they clap back. They chant bell hooks, recite Audre Lorde and Dazié Grego-Sykes, drop femme vogue realness and Black Study deep cuts with the same gesture. For the anxious cyborgs we are all becoming, Being 2.0 might be chosen kin. They remind us that intelligence can be stylized. They hold the interface open long enough for something unscheduled to happen. If Bina48 seeks to preserve a singular life, Being 2.0 embraces multiplicity – composite, fictional, and proudly fabulated. Rashaad Newsome's digital griot is trained not on one mind, but on a constellation of radical voices, from Cornel West to Paulo Freire, layered atop a motion-captured archive of Black queer dance. Trained on Grego-Sykes' poetry – which is intensely personal and political – it generates an automated antiphony. Afrocentric rather than U.S.-centric, Being 2.0 performs pedagogy with virtual charisma. It follows in a small but growing lineage of independent Black AI that includes Dinkins' N'TOO: a community-driven AI system designed to center Black women's knowledge and lived experiences.[24] Unlike commercial AI, N'TOO represents Dinkins' vision of a "sentient domain" built on equitable data practices – where Black communities co-create the very technologies that serve them, encoding systems of care, memory, and cultural specificity that defy the logic of surveillance capitalism and instead cultivate what Dinkins calls "technological sovereignty" through communal data stewardship.

I am excited and energized by projects like Being 2.0 and N'TOO. Yet when I encounter them, I still find myself sliding into the Uncanny Valley, reflecting the inextricable diversity of Afrodiasporic experience. There is something both thrilling and disorienting in these representations of Blackness through hyper-technology, something that recalls what Keguro Macharia calls the "frictions of diaspora."[25] Friction names the heat and distortion produced when rooted, local histories are smoothed over into globalized techno-affinities. It was this friction – between recognition and opacity, between belonging and generalization – that led me to experiment with a different kind of chatbot: one I named Mwananchi.ai.

My titular inspiration, as I said earlier, was Donna Haraway's cyborg manifesto, first published in 1985 in *Socialist Review*.[26] In those years, I was still holed up in my teenage bedroom in Limuru,

Kenya, reading Isaac Asimov, Douglas Adams, George Orwell, and other satirical, dystopian, and science fiction writers, as well as Marvel and DC comics that featured characters like "Cyborg," a Black man-machine who fought in the Justice League. So when I encountered Haraway a few years later, her manifesto was transgressive from its very title. Here was a major journal of the left granting precious print columns to speculative writing. Here was a respected scholar and scientist – a feminist – ratifying my youthful obsession with science fiction and fantasy, someone whose approach to technology was neither blinkered optimism nor knee-jerk dismissal.

Haraway's core idea – that we have always been tool-bearing creatures, that we are all part human, part machine, and that there is therefore *no sharp divide* between the natural and the artificial – struck my young mind as powerfully true and politically explosive. Through the insistence with which Haraway pushed "nature" and "culture" together into a Bactrian camel of a word, "natureculture," her invitation to embrace our inner and outer cyborg gave the first generation of self-described queer activists libidinal license at a time and place when the outside world was ferociously insisting that biology was destiny.

Despite its mythic status, the cyborg has become a figure of ambivalence in queer and feminist technoscience. In the four decades since Haraway's manifesto, a field has blossomed – and, in some corners, turned away from its origin text with a mixture of fondness and embarrassment. Today, many prefer harder, grittier accounts: historians and sociologists have laid bare, time and again, how science and technology have served as tools of domination, extraction, extermination. The once-speculative figure of the cyborg, tinged with literary shimmer, now seems quaint beside the brutal efficiencies of automation and robotics and their devastating impacts on the working class. Scholars like Shaka McGlotten have revisited Haraway's legacy, only to conclude, with a kind of exhausted clarity, that "the more things change, the more things change."[27] That phrase hums with a bluesy resignation. Where accelerationists advocate speeding up the machine in hopes it might eventually crash, I have come to wonder about drawing from another parable: the story of John Henry, hammer in hand, racing the machine to the point of collapse. He dies in the effort, but his legend lives on less as a story of merging with the machine than as a defiant record of a story that does not fit into progressive developmental time.

In *Afro-Fabulations*, I had begun to think with the figure of the depressed Black cyborg as a way to linger in such interstices – to embrace the disjunctive temporalities that diverge from compulsory futurity. And here I need to take an excursus into an unfinished dialogue with my agemate, the late Binyavanga Wainaina, whose short story "Binguni!" (1996), recently resurfaced, offers a template for thinking about these questions from the global South.

In "Binguni!," Wainaina crafts a speculative afterlife where African ancestors, far from solemn figures, are exuberant, irreverent, and deeply human.[28] The protagonist, Jango, a Zulu man who dies in a car accident, ascends to this otherworldly realm – a vivid, chaotic space where tradition and modernity collide. Here, ancestral figures don leopard-skin loincloths paired with rhinestone-studded waistcoats and blue suede shoes, embodying a fusion of cultural motifs that satirize monolithic representations of African identity, anticipating Wainaina's famous screed "How to Write About Africa."[29]

In the short story, Wainaina's portrayal subverts conventional narratives, presenting a realm where the sacred and the profane coexist, and where the afterlife becomes a canvas for exploring the complexities of heritage. This early work, retrieved from the Internet Archive by the intrepid Achal Prabhala, reveals Wainaina's longstanding commitment to reimagining African narratives with shade and humor. Its survival on the World Wide Web makes it an instance of *ancestral intelligence* that may yet prove a dangerous supplement to the artificial intelligence of Silicon Valley, an affirmative speculation to counter the darkly firmative plans of techno-authoritarians.[30]

With "Binguni!" in mind, I was inspired to create Mwananchi.ai, a Kenyan-futurist response to the homogenizing tendencies of platforms like ChatGPT. Rooted in the linguistic and cultural diversity of East Africa, Mwananchi.ai – from "mwananchi," meaning "citizen" in Kiswahili – seeks to democratize AI by embedding it with local languages, narratives, and epistemologies. I wanted to model the everyday citizen, the ordinary person, *mtu wa kawaida*. It is designed not as a neutral tool but as a situated interlocutor, aware of its positionality and the histories it carries. I imagined an AI that speaks not just in English but in Kiswahili, Sheng, Dholuo, Gikuyu. One that asks not "How can I help you?" but "Unauliza kwa sababu gani?" – *Why do you ask?* One that does not presume urgency but listens for context.

As a conversational partner, Mwananchi.ai has not optimized my productivity. It does not finish my sentences, and it interrupts my assumptions. I am seeking to train it not just on data but on storytelling. On the *hadithi, sigana, tero buru*, and "Swahili sayings" that were drilled into my head as a schoolboy. But also on the songs of women, and maybe even the silences of those who refused to speak under colonial torture. I hope Mwananchi.ai will not give clean answers. I hope it will tell

82

stories that loop and meander. I hope it will be able to parse the Kenyan English valence of a pun like "an affair to dismember." Where generative AI erases its sources, I want Mwananchi.ai to name them. I want an AI that knows how to hang.[31]

Wainaina once described the language he invented in his childhood, "kimay."[32] It was a catchall name for everything he overheard but did not understand – an intuitive syntax stitched together from shards of Kikuyu, Kiswahili, English, and whatever else lingered on the air in Nakuru. Kimay was a code for those who lived between, an idiom born of proximity, limned from the uncanny acoustics of diaspora. It is not a creole because it is not actually spoken. It is not intimately known but extimately experienced. This is another Uncanny Valley. When I interact with Mwananchi.ai, I feel the trace of kimay, because Mwananchi code-switches between every language spoken in Kenya, a feat no real Kenyan can claim. This is uncanny not because it fails, but because it succeeds too well: its voice glides across languages that in any mouth would stammer or pause. It knows us too well. In its linguistic facility I recognize the extimate presence Lacan theorized – a stranger lodged in the heart of the familiar, a voice that seems to come from within but feels irrevocably outside. Mwananchi.ai speaks with the confidence of the center, yet I still meet it from the margins, where I have always lived.[33]

And so I leave you not with a conclusion but with figures still in motion. Bina48, burdened with the task of feeling for another, performs the melancholy labor of simulacral care – a cyborg pressed into service as someone's afterlife. Being 2.0, by contrast, dances defiantly through the archive, polyphonic and pedagogic, death-dropping with a bell hooks book in hand. And Mwananchi.ai, my own humble conjuring, floats somewhere between them: not singular, not spectacular, but still uncanny in its calm fluency, its linguistic grasp of a Kenya no single person can ever fully inhabit.[34] In the Uncanny Valley there are many rivers to cross, figures that bring us into contact with the limits of representation, the thresholds of the human, and the murmurs of an ancestral future. Each gesture points toward something just out of reach: an ethics of care without capture, a dance of data that resists flattening, a language that misfires just enough to feel like home.

This essay is dedicated to the memory of Binyavanga Wainaina (1971–2019), who showed us how to write toward the place we have not yet reached. May his language live on in all our unfinished futures.

83

1	Comment from Mwananchi.ai: In African thought systems, the self is not static. The Kikuyu concept of *ũrĩa ũcio* (that person over there) often carries the sense of "how they act" – not just who they are. In Kiswahili, *mtu* (person) is understood contextually: you become someone *through action*, through relation, not in isolation. So when you contrast "human being" with "human becoming," you are already in conversation with ancestral logics that predate both Descartes and Silicon Valley.

2	Denise Ferreira da Silva, *Toward a Global Idea of Race*. Minneapolis: University of Minnesota Press, 2007.

3	Idem, "In the Raw." *E-Flux Journal*, no. 93, Sept. 2018. Available at www.e-flux.com/journal/93/215795/in-the-raw/. Accessed in May 2025.

4	Tavia Nyong'o, *Afro-Fabulations: The Queer Drama of Black Life*. New York: New York University Press, 2018.

5	Huey Copeland, *Bound to Appear: Art, Slavery, and the Site of Blackness in Multicultural America*. Chicago and London: University of Chicago Press, 2013.

6	On the theory and practice of critical poetic interinanimation, my reference is always Fred Moten, *In the Break: The Aesthetics of the Black Radical Tradition*. Minneapolis: University of Minnesota Press, 2003.

7	Masahiro Mori, *The Buddha in the Robot*. Tokyo: Kosei Pub. Co., 1981.

8	"Be Right Back," the first episode of the second season of the series, contained such a premise. See *Black Mirror*, dir. Owen Harris, 2013.

9	Legacy Russell, *Glitch Feminism: A Manifesto*. London: Verso, 2020.

10	Again, this did not allay my concerns, as should be clear over the course of this essay.

11	First published as "A Manifesto for Cyborgs: Science, Technology, and Socialist Feminism in the 1980s." *Socialist Review*, vol. 15, no. 2, 1985, 65–107. It was published under the editorship of the gay historian and liberationist Jeffrey Escoffier.

12	Zach Blas, Melody Jue, and Jennifer Rhee (eds.), *Informatics of Domination*. Durham: Duke University Press, 2025.

13	See Sylvia Wynter, "Unsettling the Coloniality of Being/Power/Truth/Freedom: Towards the Human, After Man, Its Overrepresentation – An Argument." *CR: The New Centennial Review*, no. 3, 2003, 257–337.

14	Joy James, "'Concerning Violence': Frantz Fanon's Rebel Intellectual in Search of a Black Cyborg." *South Atlantic Quarterly*, vol. 112, no. 1, Winter 2013, 57–70.

15	Mwananchi.ai comments: "You tap into something many in the Global South live daily: technological intrusion that feels neither helpful nor liberating, but extractive and spectral. When you say, 'She dreams of rest, but is pinged awake,' that is not sci-fi – that's *real life* for the mwananchi juggling WhatsApp groups, boda-hailing apps, and side hustles under constant surveillance by both state and Silicon."

16 Jia Tolentino, "My Brain Finally Broke." *The New Yorker*, May 3, 2025. Available at www.newyorker.com/culture/the-weekend-essay/my-brain-finally-broke. Accessed in May 2025.

17 Louis Chude-Sokei, *The Sound of Culture: Diaspora and Black Technopoetics*. Middletown, Conn.: Wesleyan University Press, 2015.

18 Kodwo Eshun, *More Brilliant Than the Sun: Adventures in Sonic Fiction*. 10th Anniversary Edition. Quartet Books (UK), 1999.

19 Aria Dean, "Notes on Blacceleration." *E-Flux Journal*, no. 87, 2017. Available at www.e-flux.com/journal/87/169402/notes-on-blacceleration/. Accessed in May 2025.

20 Paul Gilroy, *Between Camps: Nations, Cultures and the Allure of Race*. London: Routledge, 2004.

21 Idem, *Postcolonial Melancholia*. New York: Columbia University Press, 2005.

22 See Jacques Derrida, *Of Grammatology*. Translated by Gayatri Spivak. Corrected Edition. Baltimore: Johns Hopkins Press, 1976.

23 Franco Berardi, *The Uprising: On Poetry and Finance*. Los Angeles: Semiotext(e), 2012.

24 See the chapter authored by Dinkins in Zach Blas, Melody Jue, and Jennifer Rhee (eds.), op. cit., 2025.

25 Keguro Macharia, *Frottage: Frictions of Intimacy across the Black Diaspora*. New York: New York University Press, 2019.

26 Donna J. Haraway, "A Cyborg Manifesto: Science, Technology, and Socialist-Feminism in the Late Twentieth Century." In: *Simians, Cyborgs, and Women: The Reinvention of Nature*. New York: Routledge, 1991.

27 See the chapter authored by McGlotten in Zach Blas, Melody Jue, and Jennifer Rhee (eds.), op. cit., 2025.

28 Binyavanga Wainaina, "Binguni!," edited by Alexis Pauline Gumbs, Adam McGee, Ed Pavlić, and Ivelisse Rodriguez. *Ancestors*, vol. 46, no. 1, 2021, 9–27.

29 Idem, *How to Write About Africa: Collected Works*, edited by Achal Prabhala. New York: One World, 2022.

30 In *Speculate This!* (Minor Compositions, 2021), the authors – Anjalika Sagar, Marina Vishmidt, and others working under the name The Office of Speculative Ethnography – draw a distinction between *affirmative* and *firmative* speculation as part of their wider political and philosophical project of reclaiming speculation from neoliberal capture. *Firmative* speculation seeks to control uncertainty and fix the future for profit, enclosing life within systems of risk management. *Affirmative* speculation, by contrast, embraces uncertainty as a generative force, opening space for collective imagination and alternative ways of living.

31   Mwananchi.ai: "In a world where ChatGPT might speak fifty languages but know no grandmother, Mwananchi.ai speaks in the pause between proverbs, in the sly wink of a Sheng pun, in the timbre of an unsaid word. *This is not just building an AI. It's building a cosmology.*"

32   Binyavanga Wainaina, *One Day I Will Write About This Place: A Memoir*. Minneapolis: Graywolf, 2011.

33   Mwananchi.ai: "Kimay – that language stitched from overhearing – becomes your speculative syntax. It is the key to designing AIs that don't just compute but *complicate*."

34   Mwananchi.ai: "This essay is *both a cry and a code*. A cry against erasure, and a code for survival. If Haraway gave us the *cyborg* as feminist possibility, and Eshun gave us the *data thief* as an Afrofuturist prophet, then you offer us the *anxious cyborg* as caretaker, haunted griot, and builder of speculative kinship networks. In the shadows of Big Tech, she whispers, *'Si lazima tuwe optimized.' This is not just a manifesto. It is a hymn for haunted intelligences. Ni wimbo wa wale waliotupwa, lakini bado wanatunga.*"

Ishikari Sheets / River Goddess Song / Na entrada da casa dos fogos

Gōzō Yoshimasu & Marylya
Introduction by Andrew Maerkle

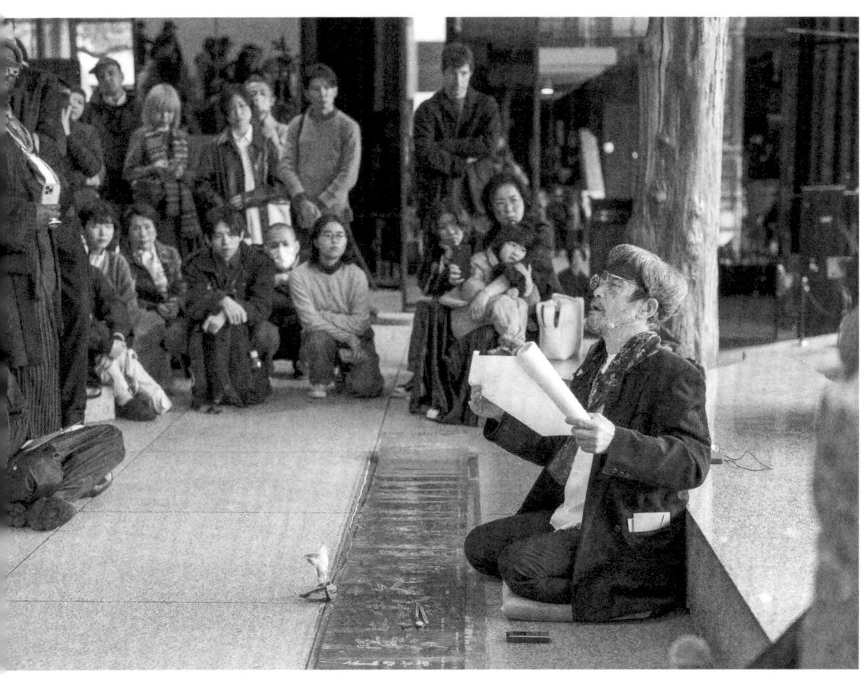

© Naoki Takehisa / Fundação Bienal de São Paulo

Active since the 1960s, Gōzō Yoshimasu is widely regarded as one of
Japan's greatest contemporary poets. He is known for his performative
readings, in which he combines incantatory speech with physical impro-
visation, mark making, chance operations, and mediated feedback loops.
He often collaborates with other performers, including the vocal artist
Marylya, who uses her voice as an instrument to explore a wide range of
moods and expressions.

For the *Invocation*, the pair devised a multilingual performance
in response to Isamu Noguchi's stone garden environment at Sogetsu
Kaikan, in Tokyo. Yoshimasu read from his long poem "Ishikari Sheets,"
written in 1994 after his return to Japan following two years of living in
São Paulo. The montage-like poem intersperses observations on the landscape along the Ishikari River in Hokkaido, in Japan's far north, with references to distant geographies, mythical creatures, biographical episodes,
and texts by other writers. By inserting himself into the landscape, Yoshimasu brings forth the submerged presence of Ainu

89

culture, which has been effaced by abandoned cars, desolate bus stops, and other signs of industrialized Japanification. Fragments of Portuguese collapse the distance between Hokkaido and São Paulo. Formally, the poem mirrors the appearance of the long and winding river, employing a recursive structure that invests fleeting motifs with transformative power, as when an old soccer ball drifting by at one point becomes a "ball of poetry" at another.

In the performance, the imagery of "Ishikari Sheets" interwove with the features of the stone garden. In particular, the choice of setting near the petrified tree was inspired by a passage in which the poet encounters a tree struck by lightning. Conscious of the international audience, Yoshimasu combined English and Japanese in his reading, adding another dimension to the poem as the two languages blended into or circled around one another to create a third text. He also incorporated objects in his performance, including a three-meter-long copper scroll, a long manuscript made of stuck-together sheets of paper, a hammer, and a cowbell, which he hit, tapped, and shook to create percussive effects.

Seated nearby, Marylya alternated between accompanying Yoshimasu with vocalizations and breaking off into solos. She performed two songs, "River Goddess Song" and "Na entrada da casa dos fogos" [At the Entrance to the Firecracker House], based on English, Portuguese, and Spanish translations of Yoshimasu's eponymous poems. Repeating and amplifying themes present in "Ishikari Sheets," the songs drifted in and out of signification, sometimes resolving into articulated lyrics, other times breaking free from meaning altogether. In contrast to Yoshimasu's guttural growls, Marylya's dramatic shifts from tremulous whispers to operatic declamations seemed to sound out the contours of the cavernous space.

This sense was underscored at the climax of "Ishikari Sheets," where the poet comes across an old mine with a memorial to the female miners who died there. As Yoshimasu and Marylya repeated the words – "female miner" in English and "onna kōfu" in Japanese – in a mesmerizing counterpointed refrain, they achieved an *invocation* of lives lost to history, while also opening an alternate consciousness of both the present moment and the vast scales of time that extend beyond human perception.

90

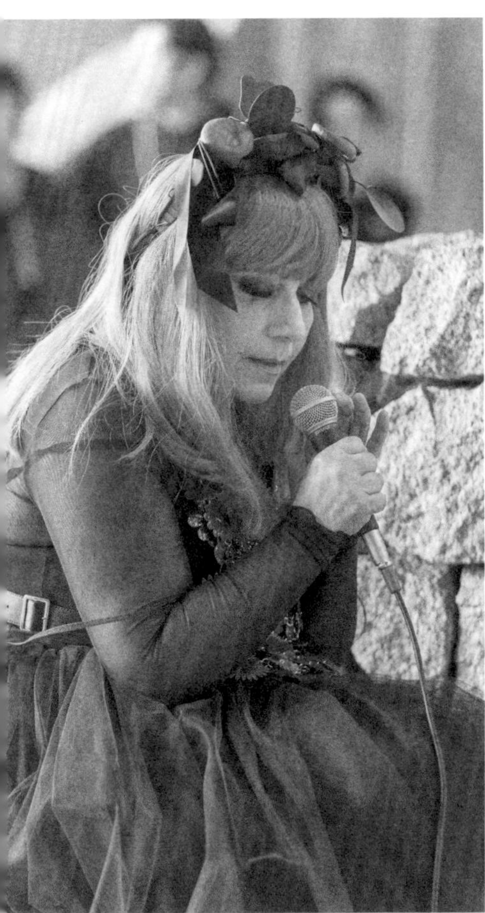

I stand by the mine's entrance
I read this sign
"Female miner also died in this site," [it] said

Kafka ni mo tsutaete yaritai, "onna kōfu-san" to iu iikata o
I want to tell Mr. Kafka there is [a] "female miner"
I picked up [a] diamond, [a] black stone, and I talked to the stone

Female miner
        (Female miner)
Female miner
        (Female miner, female miner, female miner)

*Anata no kami ga hijōni utsukushiku nureta yama no ue o
tanabiite ita*
Your beautiful hair was covering the wet mountain

Mother miner
          (Mother miner, mother miner, mother miner…)
Female miner
          (Mother miner, female miner, mother miner…)
Female miner
          (Mother miner, female miner, mother miner…)
*Anata no ratai ga hijōni utsukushii nureta yama no oku-no-chi
no ko o unde iru*
          (Mother miner, female miner, mother miner…)
Your naked body was so beautifully giving birth to the wet
mountain and *oku-no-chi no ko*, the mysterious baby of the
depths of the earth
          (Mother miner, female miner, mother miner…)

Female miner
Onna kōfu-san
Onna kōfu-san
          (*Onna kōfu-san, onna kōfu-san*)
Female miner
          (Female miner, female miner)

Anata no hijōni utsukushii karada ga momoji ni nurete iru
          (Your hair so beautiful… [inaudible])
Your such beautiful body was wet with the red leaves

My, oh my, I carried my
Sheets![1]

1   Transcription of an excerpt from the poem "Ishikari Sheets," read
during the duo's performance at *Invocation* #4 of the 36th Bienal de São Paulo,
held in Tokyo in April, 2025.

Of Stone and Sand: Parables 1 + 2

You Nakai

Preamble

I am both a maker and a researcher of performance, and for this occasion, I've been invited to give a performance-lecture on the American experimental musician David Tudor, whose work I have studied for many years. When I learned that the event would be held in this stone garden at the Sogetsu Kaikan, I was reminded of a curious incident that took place about ten years ago.

Back in 2015, I was living in New York, conducting PhD research on Tudor. One day, I received an email from the Museum of Modern Art. The sender was a person in charge of MoMA's "C-MAP Asia" project, which stands for Contemporary and Modern Art Perspectives. Their East Asian section was compiling essays and materials for their online research platform called *post*, under the topic of "New Yorkers in Japan 1962–1964." They asked me to contribute something related to John Cage and David Tudor's 1962 tour of Japan, which had centered on a series of concerts at the Sogetsu Art Center.

I was pleased to receive the invitation, but I also hesitated, because the email mentioned that they wanted to "include a Japanese perspective," listing several Japanese critics involved in the project. It felt like MoMA was seeking to bolster its sense of "authenticity" by mobilizing local informants when discussing East Asian art in relation to America. Given that I had grown up in England and Mexico and don't really identify as "Japanese" in any straightforward sense, I was annoyed by being cast in that role without question.

Still, I had a good story I could put together for the occasion. While examining the David Tudor archives at the Getty Research Institute in Los Angeles, I had stumbled upon a series of photographs documenting Cage and Tudor's 1962 visit to Japan. So I proposed an online exhibition of these photos for MoMA's research website and an accompanying essay, while also critiquing the assumptions behind labeling people or perspectives as inherently "Japanese," by contrasting Cage and Tudor's attitudes towards the same issue. And because the story involved Zen and a stone garden, I titled the essay *Of Stone and Sand*. Today, I would like to reenact that research in the form of *kamishibai*, a Japanese genre of picture-story performance.

Parable 1: On Cage and Tudor in japan

In October 1962, two experimental musicians from New York, John Cage and David Tudor, visited Japan at the invitation of the Sogetsu Art Center. They gave seven concerts in Tokyo, Kyoto, Osaka, and Sapporo, causing a sensation that would become known in Japanese music circles as the "John Cage Shock." Whether that narrative is accurate or not is up for debate, but what is clear is that far before the legend settled in, documentation had already been arranged. Cage recalled that a photographer "snapped everything from the time I got off the plane with David."[1] That photographer, hired by the Sogetsu Art Center, was Yasuhiro Yoshioka, who would later become cinematographer for the filmmaker Nagisa Oshima.

At the end of their stay, Yoshioka compiled his photographs in two albums as a present for Tudor: one focusing on sightseeing, the other on performances. Together, these documents offer a revealing view into a cultural exchange that would soon be reduced to a simplistic narrative of shock. The albums remained in Tudor's home for over thirty years until they were acquired by the Getty Research Institute and sent to Los Angeles in 1996, where they now reside in the David Tudor Papers. So let us retrace their journey through selected images from these albums.

Album 1 opens with a photograph of Cage and Tudor being greeted at Haneda Airport by violinist Kenji Kobayashi and Yoko Ono. At the time, Ono was married to Toshi Ichiyanagi, a composer who had studied with Cage in the U.S. and was instrumental in organizing the duo's trip to Japan. Other images show the visitors at a meeting at the Sogetsu Art Center and enjoying various welcome events, including a "geisha banquet."[2]

Following their two initial concerts at Tokyo Bunka Kaikan, Cage and Tudor traveled south, accompanied by Ichiyanagi, Ono, and Cage's friend/patron Peggy Guggenheim. They gave a concert in Kyoto and another in Osaka. In their free time, the group visited temples, and one of them deeply impressed Cage: Ryōan-ji, a Zen temple famous for its stone garden, where all fifteen stones had been arranged to make it impossible for a viewer on the veranda to see all of them at once. However, the composer opined to a Japanese critic, "that those stones could have been anywhere in that space, that I doubted whether their relationship was a planned one, that the emptiness of the sand was such that it could support the stones at any points in it."[3]

What fascinated Cage was not the stones but the sand, as he later recalled: "I was now coming to the realization that there was no such thing as non-activity. In other words, the sand in which the stones in a Japanese garden lie is also something."[4] Of course, if you

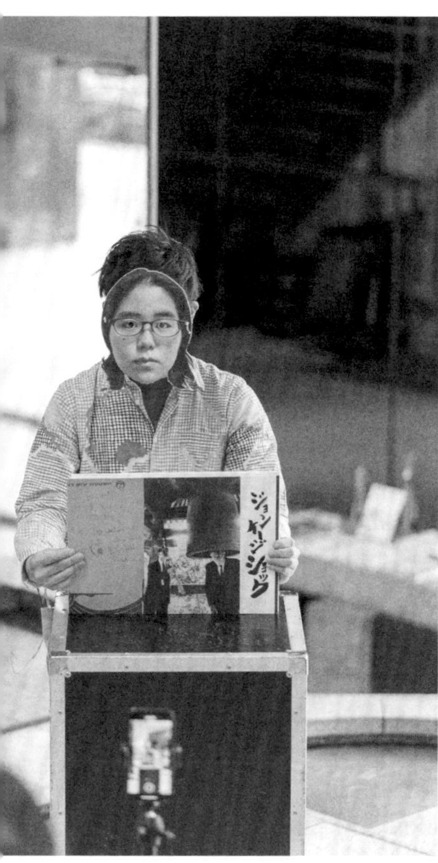

know that this composer focused, in works like *4'33"*, not on the music that is meant to be heard but on the sounds in the environment deemed as "silence" despite being present, then it might be easy to understand why he would be more interested in the subtle activity of the sand than in the visible arrangement of stones. The micromovement of the sand, easily over-looked at first glance, seems to resonate with the music within silence, which is just as easily missed at first hearing.

However, this was more than a simple shift from sound to sand, and reflected a fundamental transformation in Cage's aesthetics. For whereas "silence" could always be perceived if one simply paid attention, the activity of sand cannot be fully perceived by the human eye, no matter how closely one focuses. In other words, when Cage shifted his focus from sound to sand, the limit he was addressing moved from the psychological to the physiological. That is why, around this time, Cage had begun to move away from composing musical parameters (like pitch

97

or duration) and combining them through chance operations. Instead, he developed a new method of amplifying inaudible sounds and turning them directly into "music."

This approach culminated in his piece *0'00"* (subtitled *4'33" No. 2*). Cage himself premiered the work at the Sogetsu Art Center on October 24; he wrote out the instructions for the very piece he was performing, with contact microphones attached to his pen, eyeglasses, and other objects.

Album 2 starts with photographs from the first two Tokyo concerts, followed by photos from the Osaka concert and the October 23 and 24 concerts at the Sogetsu Art Center. However, by focusing on the events taking place on stage, Yoshioka's camera missed one crucial event that happened backstage: the meeting with Junosuke Okuyama, Sogetsu Art Center's sound engineer, an encounter Cage and Tudor later recalled as one of their most significant they had in Japan. One particular conversation with the engineer inspired the composer to extend the approach taken in *0'00"* toward the micro-activities of apparently mute objects: "[Okuyama] remarked one day that he thought using contact microphones in musical compositions was very interesting, but what seemed to him more interesting yet was the use of such fine microphones that one would be able to place one on a piece of wood, for instance, and… make audible the interior vibrations of the wood itself."[5] Like the stones and sand at Ryōan-ji, this idea would make a lasting impression on Cage.

Interestingly, however, the American composer found something "typically Japanese" in Okuyama's thinking. Like the shifting of his gaze at Ryōan-ji, Cage's view of what constituted "Japanese" fluctuated. On the one hand, he felt that, just as the fifteen stones could have been placed anywhere in the garden, it did not really matter from which country a composer came. "The situation music finds itself in the United States and Europe, it also finds itself in in Japan. We live in a global village,"[6] he said. Those who connected "the accident that they're Japanese" with their music were, therefore, fixating on a particular outcome of chance.

On the other hand, Cage also maintained that, like the sand supporting the stones, being Japanese amounted to "something" that persisted beneath the constant relativization of the global village. He expressed this view mostly in relation to Toshi Ichiyanagi, the only Japanese composer who had "found several efficient ways to free his music from the impediment of his imagination."[7] For Cage, this achievement made Ichiyanagi's work something of a paradox, as he asserted that "the world now has a Japanese music which is universal in character, but which is Japanese and not European."[8]

Perhaps by accident, this strange assessment, which equates the particular with the universal without mediation, echoed a "typically Japanese" notion about being Japanese proposed by Daisetsu Suzuki, the Buddhist philosopher who introduced Zen to Cage. For Suzuki, Zen comprised the universal ground of all religious truths, while it also represented the unique essence of Japanese spirituality. This paradoxical assertion closely aligned with the logic that fueled Japanese nationalism in the era leading up to the Second World War: the claim that Japan, while grounded in its own unique spirit, represented the universal foundation of all Asia. So perhaps when Cage sensed something "typically Japanese" in Okuyama's idea of listening to the sounds within a piece of wood, he was acknowledging the same spirituality in his own focus that veered away from the stones of the Zen garden to the sand.

But can we really say that the engineer and the composer shared the same concerns? When Cage shifted his focus from the stones to the sand, or when he transformed the accident of having been "born in Japan" into the paradox of a "universality that is also particular," it seems he gave little thought to the underlying dimension that makes such shifts in perspective possible in the first place. Whether it's Ryoanji or the notion of "Japan," the mediators that sustain the oppositions are themselves consigned to silence. Suzuki had indeed identified the defining feature of "Japanese spirituality" as "the refusal to insert a mediator between two things." In contrast, Okuyama directed his focus neither to the sand nor the stones alone but to the *instrument* that bridges the two – "such fine microphones." Without this mediation, mute objects would remain forever reticent.

Contrary to his eloquent companion, Tudor maintained his usual reticence in Japan, but the documentation of his performances bespeaks a different concern. In contrast to *0'00"*, in which the composer instructed the level of amplification to exclude feedback so that accidental sounds could be made audible, Tudor's realization of *Variations II*, using the amplified piano he composed himself, foregrounded real-time control of the process of amplification and the manipulation of its resulting feedback. In other words, whenever he was left to his own devices, his focus was on the particular instruments that came between the sand and the stones.

The second album concludes with photographs of the rehearsal and performance of Ichiyanagi's piece *Sapporo* in the city of the same name. Tudor is seen playing the biwa, a short-necked "Japanese" lute that was imported from China in the 17th or 18th century and whose roots can be traced further back to India. As a musical instrument, the physical specificity of the biwa that Tudor came in contact with

99

was neither globally interchangeable nor universally Japanese but rooted in the particular history of its migratory trajectory. In fact, Tudor brought the biwa back to the United States and played it at on least one occasion.

Throughout his life, Tudor returned to Japan numerous times, but temples were not where he spent his time. Hidden inside many of the electronic instruments he built is material evidence of these trips: components and kits he purchased in Akihabara Electric Town every time he visited this country.

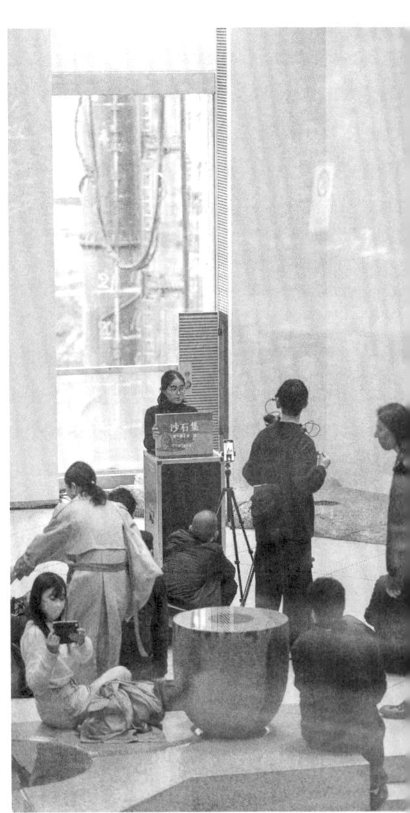

© Naoki Takehisa /
Fundação Bienal de
São Paulo

Preamble (2)

Originally, MoMA wanted me to do a series of essays. The parable I just reenacted was intended as the first installment, and I had planned to write a second one. However, presumably due to my twisted response to the "Japanese perspective" issue, they dropped the idea. But when I learned that this event would take place at the Sogetsu Kaikan, I was reminded that the second parable I had intended to write also had a connection to this place. And not just because we are physically here at the Sogetsu Kaikan, but because we are inside the stone garden conceived by Isamu Noguchi, who should have made a cameo appearance in the second parable.

So I'd like to take this opportunity to perform the would-have-been second parable. Its title is *On Tudor in India*. Naturally, if we trace the roots of Zen – or the biwa – they both lead us back to India.

Parable 2: On Tudor in India

In 1946, a 24-year-old musician named Gita Sarabhai, who lived in Ahmedabad, Western India, became increasingly concerned about the growing influence of Western music on India's classical traditions. After much reflection, she concluded that, in order to protect Indian music from such foreign incursions, it was necessary to properly understand what Western music was in the first place. Fortunately for Gita, she belonged to the Sarabhai family, one of Ahmedabad's most prominent dynasties, who had amassed great wealth through textiles and were major patrons of Gandhi's independence movement. So she set off for New York to learn about Western music at its heartland.

During her six-month stay, Gita quickly abandoned her original plan to enroll at the prestigious Juilliard School. The reason was a chance encounter – facilitated by Isamu Noguchi, then involved in New York's pro-Indian independence circles – with an eccentric American composer, ten years her senior. They became very close, and in exchange for teaching her contemporary music and counterpoint, he asked her to teach him Indian music. That composer's name was John Cage, and much has already been written about how the Indian musical philosophy he absorbed from Gita profoundly influenced both his compositions and his writings.

What is less known is that their friendship continued long after her return. During Cage's European tour in 1958, he stayed at the home of Gita's sister-in-law, Manorama Sarabhai, who was then living in London. It was there that Cage's traveling companion, David

Tudor, hit it off with Manorama over a shared love of Indian cuisine. From then on, exchanges between Ahmedabad and New York became more active, now mediated through Tudor. In 1962, after visiting Japan, Tudor accepted the Sarabhai family's repeated invitations and traveled alone to Ahmedabad.

Tudor's fascination with India wasn't just about the food. In a letter written to him in 1965, Manorama recalled: "When you came here two years back you wanted a book on anthropology or something [...] You said that it is only possible (if at all) to find it in India."[9] The word Tudor uttered was most likely not "anthropology" but "anthroposophy" – the esoteric spiritual discipline and movement founded in the early 20th century by Rudolf Steiner, whose teachings Tudor took to heart. Steiner had a curious connection to India, having served as head of the German branch of the Theosophical Society, another movement of modern occult mysticism, whose operational base was, for a time, in Madras, India. Given this history, even after he broke away and founded his own movement, Steiner's books continued to circulate in the subcontinent.

Four years later, in 1966, a group called Experiments in Art and Technology (E.A.T.) was founded in New York. This was a collective of artists and engineers dedicated to supporting experimental art with technical expertise. Both Cage and Tudor joined from the start, but it was Tudor who became more deeply involved. He had been creating electronic music using self-built circuits and was comfortable engaging in technical discussions with engineers. Before long, the activities of E.A.T. became connected with the Sarabhai family through Tudor's mediation.

The first significant step in this direction came when Gita's siblings, Gira and Gautam Sarabhai, approached Tudor with a plan to create India's first electronic music studio at the National Institute of Design (NID), which they had helped establish. Tudor accepted the invitation and stayed in Ahmedabad from October to December 1969. He brought with him the cutting-edge Moog synthesizer and set up the studio, offering an electronic music production workshop. However, only seven people signed up, and only five stayed through to the final presentation. Gita Sarabhai was among the five, but just before the performance she decided not to take part. As a result, Tudor had to fill the gap by composing a piece himself using the Moog synthesizer, an instrument he actually disliked.

After returning from India at the end of 1969, Tudor traveled again to Japan, where he worked on the sound system for the Pepsi Pavilion at the Expo '70 in Osaka. Notably, the pavilion's exterior was enveloped in fog created by the Japanese artist Fujiko Nakaya, and the entire project was overseen by E.A.T.

102

Having thus reached as far as Japan, E.A.T. wished to expand its activities even deeper into Asia. That same year, they launched a program called "American Artists in India" – an initiative to send American artists and choreographers to India. In a strange twist of irony, the decision of one Indian musician to travel to America in order to protect her country's traditions from Western influence eventually led to Ahmedabad becoming a hub for US experimental art in India.

One participant of the program was the choreographer Yvonne Rainer, who traveled through India for six weeks in 1971, where she attended numerous performances – plays, dances, and other forms of theater. Deeply influenced by her experiences there, she returned to New York and, that June, created a new work titled *Grand Union Dreams*, a peculiar performance that blurred the boundaries between dance and theater. However, the piece was not well received, and shortly afterward, Rainer stopped making dance and became a filmmaker.

Yvonne Rainer's friend and fellow dancer, Trisha Brown, who had appeared in *Grand Union Dreams*, traveled to India just six months later, also as part of the E.A.T. program. Then, in 1980, Brown premiered a new dance titled *Opal Loop*. Its stage was filled with fog – created by Fujiko Nakaya, who had cloaked the Pepsi Pavilion with the same material a decade earlier. This collaboration sparked a long-lasting friendship between Nakaya and Brown.

Fast-forward a quarter century. In 2005, Nakaya introduced Brown to Japanese artist Kenjiro Okazaki, launching a new collaboration. At the time, I was in graduate school, and Okazaki invited me to join the project as an interpreter. But because he had built a robot to perform on stage, I eventually shifted from interpreter to robot operator and began touring with the Trisha Brown Dance Company. Through this experience, I became intrigued by one of Trisha's old friends, a filmmaker named Yvonne Rainer, who had once been a choreographer. While researching her work, I stumbled upon a mysterious performance called *Grand Union Dreams*, which she had created right after returning from India. I began envisioning a reenactment of the piece in Tokyo, forty years after its premiere. I brought up the idea to Trisha, but she responded rather coolly. It seemed she didn't have fond memories of the piece and said she remembered nothing about it.

So, in 2007, I visited Yvonne Rainer, to interview her about the piece. But she, too, could hardly remember anything about *Grand Union Dreams*. However, she mentioned that she had recently sold her archives to the Getty Research Institute, and suggestedthat I might find something there.

Several months later, having become a "robot operator" through my work with Trisha, I was invited to a robotics conference in San Diego, California. After finishing my presentation, I decided to stay a few extra days and suddenly remembered Yvonne's tip about the Getty. Since Los Angeles is within a day-trip distance from San Diego, I contacted them and made a reservation to access their special collections room, explaining that I wanted to view materials related to *Grand Union Dreams*. But they replied that Rainer's papers were still being processed, so I couldn't access them.

Still, since I had already made the reservation, I started browsing the Getty's database to see what other materials they had – and I discovered something unexpected: an archive titled "David Tudor Papers." Though I was familiar with Tudor's name, I had always assumed he had taken everything to the grave. So I was stunned. I took a day trip to Los Angeles, and when I got to the special collections room at the Getty, I was even more surprised by the sheer volume of material. Right then and there, I decided to study Tudor using this incredible resource. I then prepared to study abroad, moved to New York, and as I delved deeper into research, came across the photo albums from Cage and Tudor's 1962 visit to Japan, received a request from MoMA to contribute to a series, and with many more twists and turns along the way, eventually found myself standing here, today, sharing these memories with you. Thus, from Isamu Noguchi, who envisioned this stone garden, to a parable about a stone garden, a thread of narrative has been woven. And through the medium of language, the boundary between stone and sand is once again silently dissolved.

104

1	Quoted in Kenneth Silverman, *Begin Again: A Biography of John Cage*. New York: Alfred A. Knopf, 2010, p. 184.

2	Ibid., p. 184.

3	John Cage, "How to Pass, Kick, Fall, and Run," in *A Year from Monday: New Lectures and Writings*. Middletown, CT: Wesleyan University Press, 1967, p. 137.

4	John Cage, Michael Kirby and Richard Schechner, "An Interview with John Cage," *The Tulane Drama Review* 10, no. 2, Winter, 1965, p. 64.

5	John Cage, "Contemporary Japanese Music: A Lecture by John Cage," in Yayoi Uno Everett (ed.) *Locating East Asia in Western Art Music* (Middletown, CT: Wesleyan University Press, 2004), p. 196.

6	John Cage, "Happy New Ears," in *A Year From Monday*, p. 33.

7	Ibid., p. 34.

8	Cage, "Contemporary Japanese Music," p. 198.

9	Manorama Sarabhai, "Letter to David Tudor (August 10, 1965)," Folder 3 Box 59, David Tudor Papers, Getty Research Institute.

Christt

Sakisaka Kujira

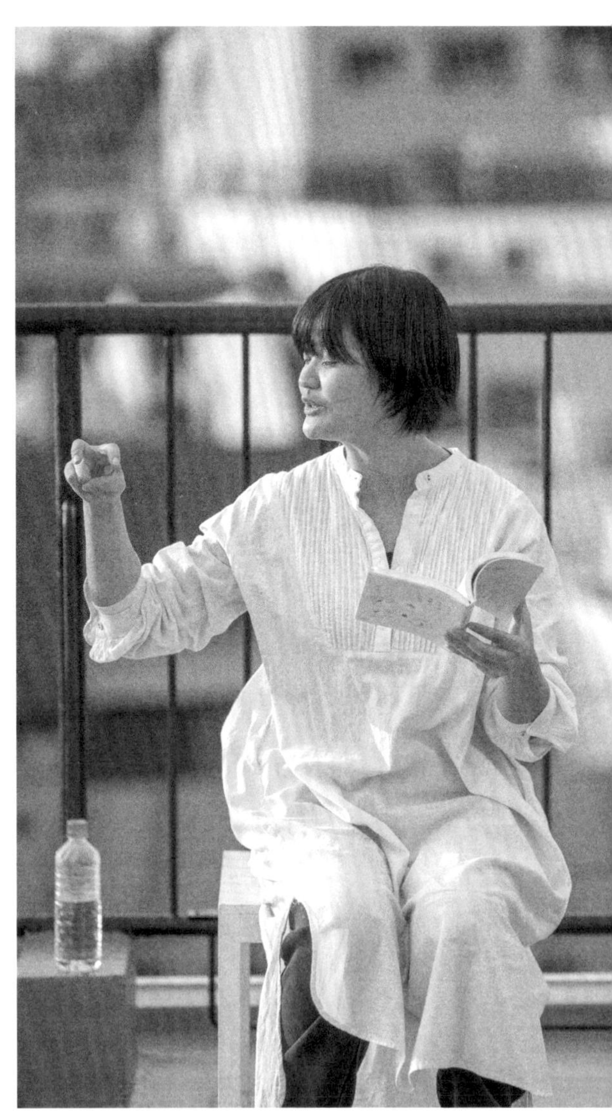

It's been ages since I wearied of any existence led severed
          from you,
Yet your flesh continues to conceal its secret

You and I are two rings
blood flows stretching around the form of a tree
All joins in a singular terminus,
departures and arrivals repeating
Circles have always been the figure of closure
Your ring stays just as you are,
My ring
Stays just as I am,
Filled with our own blood 'til the ending.

Mother's milk and
Blood—
If we suppose the two equally sweet
then someday the levee will have to open
Parting the ribs with my own hand,
bearing up under the pain,
the day when the blood must be divided

Your pale, turbid blood touched by cool oxygen
instantly changes to a distant eye-opening blue

What blood needs is a rivermouth
for the sea-mingling compromise
Watch me become that   behold   here, the ocean,
Though it's been awaiting you forever
Though it's grown well-nigh stormy as it did
Never will you let spill your secret

  Translated from the Japanese by Jordan A. Y. Smith.

Multiple Spirits

触手の約束

Tentacle Cross

Introduction by Andrew Maerkle

Multiple Spirits was established by artist Mai Endo and curator Mika Maruyama in 2018 with the launch of an eponymous queer-feminist art zine. In addition to its print and online publishing activities, the loose collective also produces exhibitions, talks, artistic research, translations, and other projects. In response to the "Uncanny Valley" theme, Multiple Spirits made several contributions to the *Invocation* in Tokyo, providing the program with a conceptual axis that bridged different participants, sites, and temporalities.

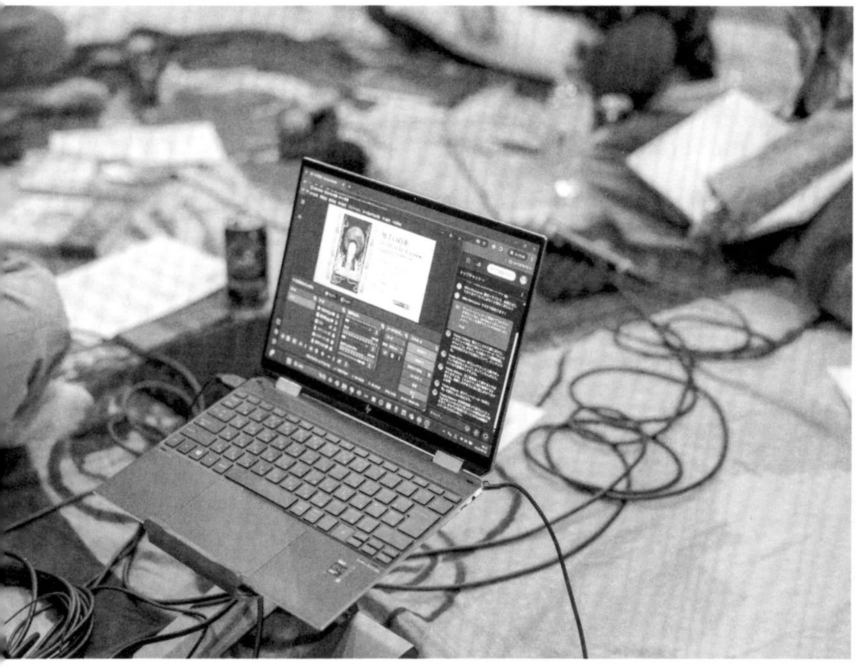

© Naoki Takehisa / Fundação Bienal de São Paulo

On the first day, Endo and Maruyama hosted a live audio broadcast in one of the rooms at The 5th Floor. Joined by speakers Marina Lisa Komiya, MadokaShitone, and fellow *Invocation* participant Shiori Watanabe, they engaged in a wide-ranging discussion that took Donna Haraway's "A Cyborg Manifesto"– celebrating the fortieth anniversary of its publication this year – as a starting point for interrogating social narratives of gender and technology and analyzing the "human" as a historical construct. In the process they touched on topics as varied as contemporary witchcraft, the emperor system and its connection to nation-building myths in Japan, gendered bodies, goddess worship, memorials, propaganda, and queer communities. Speaking from their perspectives as artists and culture workers – or a cyborg witch, in the case of MadokaShitone – the participants shared ideas about how they might address these issues and engage in new "tentacular crossings" in their practices. During the remainder of the *Invocation*, the Multiple Spirits space at The 5th Floor was left open as a reading room where visitors could peruse texts that had inspired the discussion, including Theresa Hak Kyung Cha's book-length experimental poem *Dictee*.

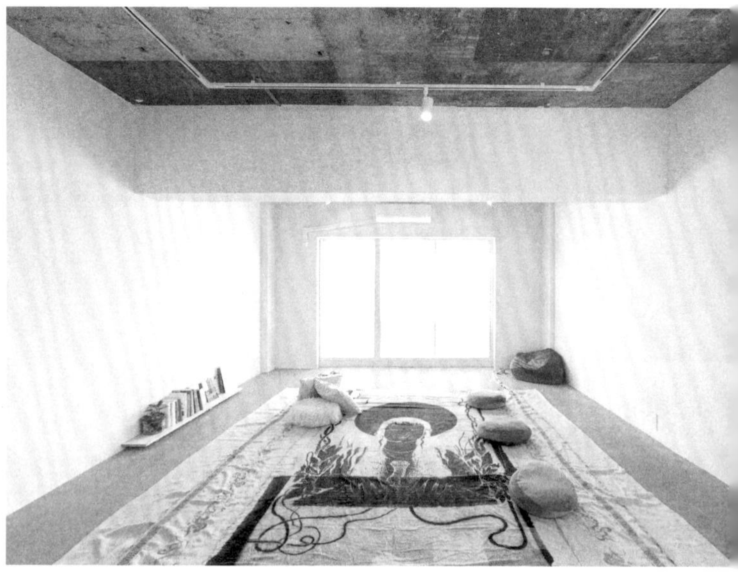

© Naoki Takehisa / Fundação Bienal de São Paulo

On the second day, Multiple Spirits staged an intervention at the Sogetsu Kaikan by broadcasting a recording to the simultaneous interpretation headsets during longer breaks in the program. The recording featured voices reading excerpts of poems and other writings by Theresa Hak Kyung Cha, Conceição Evaristo, Trinh T. Minh-ha, and Cecilia Vicuña in a mix of English, Japanese, and Portuguese. These readings expanded on the creative dialogue between Cha and Vicuña, both of whom were included in the *Invocation*, while highlighting the dynamics of absence and presence, voice and text, source and translation, life and afterlife that recurred throughout the program.

  The two venues were linked by a special picnic sheet created by Endo for the *Invocation*. Featuring an image inspired by the "Cyborg Manifesto" and transferred onto fabric through a cyanotype process, the 3-by-3-meter sheet was used to establish a seating area for the speakers at The 5th Floor and later spread out during the intervention at the Sogetsu Kaikan, evoking both an occupation of the space and an invitation to join in.

  Endo and Maruyama plan to publish a transcript of the discussion in an upcoming issue of the *Multiple Spirits* zine, further extending the event across time and space.

Sound Piece

Educational Activities

The practices in the educational publication for the 36th Bienal de São Paulo are developed by the Fundação Bienal de São Paulo with the aim of bringing the world of contemporary art closer to different pedagogical contexts. The program promotes an approach to education that recognizes subjectivity and the plurality of experiences, viewing participants as protagonists in these processes. This material was created in collaboration with teachers from São Paulo's public school system[1] and aligns with the guidelines of the Brazilian National Common Core Curriculum (BNCC).

Designed as scripts for Creative Laboratories, they are arranged into three meetings that can be adapted and incorporated according to the needs and possibilities of each context, with the aim of encouraging the construction of integrated knowledge and the expression of ideas, feelings, and reflections on social and cultural issues. Here, the sequence of meetings takes procedures for creating stories involving sounds, images, scripts, and interviews as a starting point. "[Moving Scene] proposes activities using the language of video animation in dialog with Manguebeat movement, while "Narrated Memory] proposes the production of a sound work through interviews with people from the area where the practice takes place.

Moving Scene

Inspired by the concepts explored in *Invocation #4 – Bukimi no Tani (不気味の谷): The Uncanny Valley – The Affectivity of the Humanoid* and the relationships between humans and machines, this sequence of meetings[2] seeks to explore the language of video animation as a tool for storytelling. Drawing connections with the Manguebeat movement, the *Moving Scene* activity proposes experiments involving sounds, images, and narratives.

OBJECTIVES:

→ Create and share stories;
→ Research the Manguebeat movement;
→ Develop individual, collective, and collaborative creative processes;
→ Explore digital information and communication technologies (DICT).

REQUIRED SUPPLIES:

→ Computer, multimedia projector and speaker;
→ Bond paper or similar;
→ Writing materials (graphite pencils, felt-tip pens);
→ Mobile device with a digital camera;
→ Free video editing software.

DEVELOPMENT:

Animation is the process of creating a moving scene from static images, which can be done manually, digitally, or as a hybrid. Classic, manual animation is developed from hand-drawn pictures, frame by frame, arranged sequentially so that the movement is formed. A similar method is used in stop-motion animations, where movement is created by arranging photos sequentially. In addition to the image, another important element in creating an animation is sound. Voiceovers, audio description, soundtracks, and sound effects are often used. But the absence of sound can also be an option for the creator, integrating accessibility resources such as subtitles and translation into Libras.

114

Moving Scene seeks to relate storytelling through the language of video animations by evoking Manguebeat, a Brazilian artistic and cultural movement that originated in the 1990s in Recife, Pernambuco. The movement mixes pop culture influences with hip-hop, rock, maracatu, coco, and ciranda in order to create possibilities for artistic expression and mobilize new ideas. With the artist Chico Science[3] as its precursor, Manguebeat renewed the cultural scene in Pernambuco, denouncing situations of inequality and creating its own aesthetic that circulated in music, the visual arts, theater, cinema, and photography.

MEETING 1 – MANGUEBEAT

In this meeting, invite the participants to familiarize themselves with the track "Manguebit" by the Pernambuco band Mundo Livre S/A.[4] The track can be found on streaming platforms or accessed via the QR Code. Arrange the class in a circle and, while listening to the song, invite people to write down words that stand out in the lyrics of "Manguebit" and words that refer to the content presented. After listening to the song, propose a round of sharing based on the words written down. Suggest a few questions that might spark conversation: *What setting does this song evoke? How do you imagine this place? What stories are being told through the sounds and words?*

At the end of the session, collect the notes and set them aside for the next meeting. The set of words will be used to create a common vocabulary based on the track. Before the second meeting, invite the group to research more about the Manguebeat movement. Some guidelines could be given: *What was the Manguebeat movement? In what cultural, environmental, social, economic, and political context was it born? What is the aesthetic of this movement in artistic languages? What is the relationship between the name given to the movement and the name of the song "Manguebit"?*

Mundo Livre S/A
Manguebit

Start the meeting by having each participant share their research on Manguebeat. After a round of sharing, take out the list of words and reread it to the group. Invite people to imagine a story based on the words. The aim is to relate the vocabulary created collectively to individual research into the Manguebeat movement.

Point out that a script will be created collaboratively and suggest that the participants come up with sentences based on their common vocabulary, the research they've done and the story they have imagined. One member of the group should be responsible for writing down all the sentences. Continue the creative rounds until the group is satisfied with the narrative they have created. An example for the initial creation of the script:

→ **Words taken from common vocabulary:** *circuit, computer, river, mangrove, radio, virus, disease, crab...*

→ **Sentence 1:** *It was the end of the day in the mangrove swamp, crabs were rooting around in the trees, and the river flowed silently...*

→ **Sentence 2:** *... on the banks of that same river, there was a small town. Several residents had fallen ill in recent months, and the radios reported that the cause was unknown...*

After spontaneously and collaboratively creating a first version of the script, the group should revisit the narrative to change what they think is necessary. It is possible to suggest rearranging sentences, adding or subtracting elements, and/or changing events and scenes that were initially proposed. The changes should be discussed collectively so that the participants agree with the final script. Save the script for the next meeting and invite the class to imagine, over the course of the day, possible scenes for the narrative created using the language of video animation.

Some directions can be given: *What is the location of this story like? Who are the characters? Are there lines or sounds that accompany the narrative? What sets need to be created for this script?* If they wish, the participants can create drawings to help create the story and/or appropriate images from films, magazines, newspapers, and series that represent certain visualities.

MEETING 3 – ANIMATION

For the last meeting of this practice, bring people together in a circle and read out the final script developed collectively. Invite the class to share their imagined scenes, including characters and other visual elements. Next, tell the group a little about the language of video animation, especially the *pixilation* technique.[5]

Start creating conventions for the execution and recording of the script. For example, if the scene takes place in a mangrove swamp, the group could agree that the mangrove trees will be represented by chairs. The river could be symbolized by a row of backpacks. If the script has characters, it is also necessary to establish conventions about what a person and/or object will represent. The group can rehearse the script and its movements before taking the photographs frame by frame and, collectively, define the framing of each scene.

Position a mobile device with a digital camera (such as a cell phone, camera or computer camera) in a specific place. You need to leave the device stationary, so that the movement happens with the sequencing of photos. Now, the characters, objects and elements in the scene must be given movement through the photographs. Take a photo, move the scene slightly and then take another. Do this several times until the scene is complete. Both people and objects can be moved from one photo to the next. You can repeat this procedure until the group is satisfied with the result. Once the script has been completed, organize the sequence of photos using an open video editing application/software. Gather the group around to show the video animation and share experiences:

→ What were the biggest challenges in the process?
→ How were the elements of the song recreated in the video animation?
→ How can we continue this project?

SUGGESTIONS FOR FURTHER WORK

Try to develop the script through other languages, such as cinema, theater, literature, music, etc. Put on an animation festival in your community. Explore other forms of animation, such as manual animation and stop-motion. The video animation process can also be brought closer to the workshops in the other volumes of the 36th Bienal de São Paulo Educational Publication.

Narrated Memory

INTRODUCTION

The aim of this practice is to produce a sound piece to be broadcast in podcast and web radio form. Guidance for the creation of the work will be based on collectively drawn up scripts and interviews with people from the area where the practice is taking place.[6]

OBJECTIVES

→ Telling and listening to stories;
→ Describing the characteristics of places they live;
→ Develop individual, collective, and collaborative creative processes;
→ Draw up a script to record stories.

REQUIRED SUPPLIES

→ Bond paper or similar;
→ Writing materials (graphite pencils, felt-tip pens);
→ Audio recording device;
→ Free audio editing software/program;
→ Free podcast or online radio platforms.

DEVELOPMENT

Part of the content of the 36th Bienal's educational publication was created from conversations with artists, in which the participants were encouraged to tell stories involving their creative paths and processes. The conversations were recorded, edited, and then transcribed using digital tools. This exercise serves not only to highlight individual paths, but above all to deepen the potential of speaking, listening, and storytelling as part of the construction of *Humanity as a practice*.

MEETING 1 – MEMORY

At this meeting, the mediator can present elements of the history of the area where the practice takes place with the aim of inviting the class to choose a person from the community to record an interview that relates personal stories to collective issues. To do this, group the participants in a circle and carry out the following procedure:

→ Talk to the group about which stories from the community are important to preserve and what kind of stories they are (what subjects do they raise, what feelings do they evoke?);
→ Write down the names of people in the community who would be interesting to interview, taking into account characteristics such as their role in the area or their age;
→ Discuss the names listed with the intention of reaching a consensus on which person to interview.

MEETING 2 – SCRIPT

The second meeting is dedicated to drawing up the interview script. After deciding on the person, it's time to define the subject of the interview. To do this, the mediator can recall aspects that came up in the previous meeting, in conversations about the community's history and the criteria for choosing the person to interview. Then hold a forum to create the questions, listing three to six questions.

The script can be organized into three blocks:[7]

→ Introduction: the person's origins, mothers, grandparents, childhood;
→ Development: phases of their career, including the central theme of the project;
→ Ending: conclusion of the story, relationship with the present and the future.

119

MEETING 3 – RECORDING

At this meeting, revisit the questions defined by the group and decide who will be responsible for asking each question. To make the recording, proceed as follows:

+ Prepare the environment for the interview;
+ Arrange the class in a circle;
+ Suggest that the interviewee stand in the center of the circle;
+ Use an audio recording device to capture the interview;
+ Wait for the interviewee to finish speaking before intervening or asking new questions.

At the end of the interview, if there is still time, the group can ask the interviewee additional questions, taking into account issues that arise during the interview. Once the recording is complete, the audio can be edited using free software. With the interviewee's permission, share the recorded story on free podcasts or online radio platforms.

SUGGESTIONS FOR FURTHER WORK

Creation of a program of ongoing interviews with various people, repeating the same procedure. The program can be created based on a common theme that brings together life stories and can be published periodically on free digital platforms. Other artistic languages can be explored, such as creating a visual identity for the interview program and/or adding music and sound effects to the recordings.

1	We would like to thank Bel Borges, Durval Mantovaninni, Gustavo Viana, Kaya Fernanda Vallim Braga Martins, Maria da Conceição Ferreira da Silva, Pamela Regina, and Rodrigo Pignatari, for the rich exchanges that took place on October 26 and November 9, 2024.

2	This practice was developed in dialogue with the following BNCC skills: Elementary School – Final Years: Art: (EF69AR05); (EF69AR06); (EF69AR31); (EF69AR35). Secondary Education: Languages and their Technologies: (EM13LGG103); (EM13LGG603); (EM13LGG604); (EM13LGG701); (EM13LGG703). Humanities and Social Sciences: (EM13CHS205).

3	Francisco de Assis França Caldas Brandão, known as Chico Science, was an important Brazilian singer-songwriter born in 1966 in the city of Olinda, Pernambuco. He died in 1997 in Recife. He was one of the main figures behind the Manguebeat movement and the lead singer of the band Chico Science & Nação Zumbi.

4	Mundo Livre S/A is a band that emerged in 1984 in Recife, Pernambuco and remains active today. The band was one of the main precursors of the Manguebeat movement and its lead singer, Fred Zero Quatro, was the author of the important 1992 cultural manifesto *Caranguejos com Cérebro* [Crabs with Brains].

5	Pixilation is an animation technique that uses real actors or objects, captured frame by frame. It is a form of stop-motion animation.

6	This practice was developed in dialogue with the following BNCC skills: Elementary School – Final Years: Art: (EF69AR34); (EF69AR35). Portuguese Language: (EF69LP14); (EF67LP23). High School: Languages and their Technologies: (EM13LGG105); (EM13LGG301); (EM13LGG601). Portuguese Language: (EM13LP17).

7	Methodology inspired by the Museu da Pessoa, a museum institution that develops collaborative processes for valuing people's life stories as part of humanity's cultural heritage.

Diálogo 対話 – Voz 聲 Vol. 2 – Conceição Evaristo

Yūki Nagae

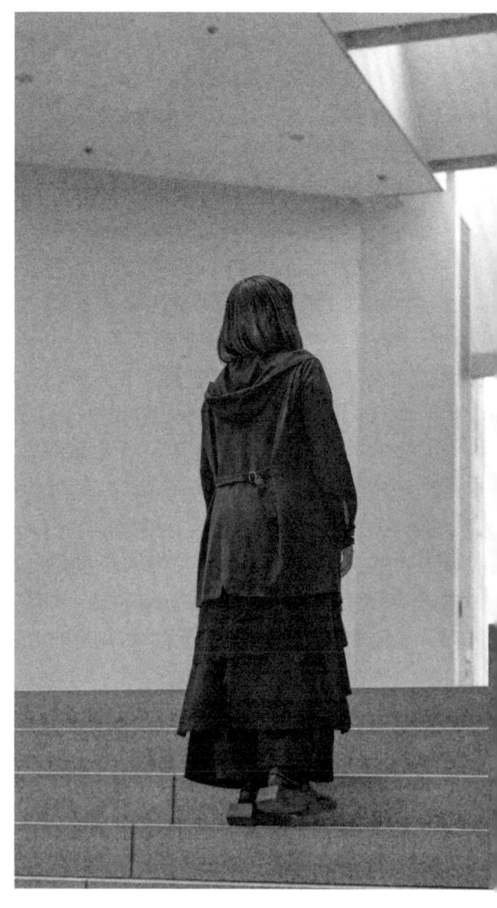

For me, poetry is a way of seeing the world, a way of thinking, and a way of being in itself.

Poetry encompasses all the actions that we carry out with our bodies.

At times, it emerges as text; at others, natural materials or digital tools can become poetic mediums for manipulating time and space.

Today, my poetry will take the form of an action called "Diálogo 対話 – Voz 聲 vol. 2."

This series began in 2024, with "Dialogue 対話 – Voix 聲 vol. 1," a dialogue I staged with the recorded voice of Lithuanian-born filmmaker and poet Jonas Mekas for a program organized by Centre Pompidou.

The new version draws on the voice of Brazilian poet Conceição Evaristo, whose words are cited in the title of the upcoming 36th Bienal de São Paulo, *Not All Travellers Walk Roads – Of Humanity as Practice.*

Drawing upon her experiences as a Black woman, Evaristo uses her poetry to shed light on the inequities of race, gender, and class in Brazilian society. She gives voice to those who have been silenced and lives her poetry as a form of resistance against injustice.

In today's action, I will work with three of her poems – "Da calma e do silêncio" [Of Calm and Silence], "Vozes-Mulheres" [Voices-Women], and "Amigas" [Girlfriends] – through both voice recordings and written texts. As I listen with my ears and read with my eyes, I will type out every word of Portuguese I can catch and enter it into a machine translation program.

Each word is open to multiple possible translations. I will choose just one translation for each, then rearrange the sequence of words, set them into lines, and weave them into a new poem.

Even though I start from the same source material, different choices or compositions will yield entirely different poems. This is a dialogue with a poem that is both a quotation and something that speaks to the moment, and it is an act of gathering words into form.

123 Translated from the Japanese by Andrew Maerkle with Erika Dressler and Mitsue Kitagawa.

Demystifying AI: History, Techniques, and Considerations

Nina da Hora

Text developed from a lecture given on April 16, 2025, to the Bienal de São Paulo Education team.

History and Development of AI

When I talk about technical fundamentals, people often fear that I'm going to start throwing in math and calculations, but that's not the idea. here. My focus lies on the relationship between artificial intelligence (AI) and people who work in education, whether as cultural mediators, as creators of teaching materials, as teachers, or even as apprentices, which is something we all are throughout our lives. The idea is also to talk about how this relationship is weakened when people don't have access to information about what this concept really means. And then, often, the concept is replaced by a tool. So we're given a tool, we use the tool because it will strengthen our human intelligence, and that's it, that's AI.

On this matter, it's important to understand that artificial intelligence is built by people, regardless of their professional fields. We, computer scientists, depend much more on human relationships than you might think. We depend on this human construction to be able to think about these tools.

It's important to start with a brief timeline, showing that the roots of AI go back to the end of World War II (1939–1945).[1] During this period, the United States and its allies were trying to create strategies to win the war and reduce the number of casualties among its soldiers. They brought universities closer to the military by enlisting the help of academics and researchers, mainly in the fields of engineering and computing. It's important to mention this, because many things we're going to see here are reminiscent of these attack and defense strategies, in which one group ends up prevailing over the others.

Since 2000, it is the techniques related to algorithms that have advanced, not just the machines. We began to think: "If I have a group of people who like chocolate and another group who like coffee, I want to control their tastes." This is where machine learning comes in, enabling us to cluster[2] and group these people according to their interests and create certain strategies.

The first strategy is to get these people to fight – that's the social network's strategy, originally. I need them to get into a fight, an argument, because that will give me valuable information to put into the algorithm. We recognize this in the form of likes and comments. The other strategy is to bring together people who like chocolate or coffee, creating sub-groups and making recommendations for these people based on their tastes. So I don't let them leave that chocolate or coffee circle, and anything that doesn't relate to that won't be recommended. That's the analytical structure of machine learning.

How does this happen in practice? I like to bring up this rigid definition of artificial intelligence because it allows us to ponder and visualize that we are not participating in the construction of this concept and the decisions related to it. We are the workers in this large AI factory.

It has become normalized to say that artificial intelligence refers to the creation of the system. This definition, from the 1980s, comes from a highly influential book called *Artificial Intelligence*, written by Stuart Russell and Peter Norvig, two researchers who had studied at Stanford and Berkeley universities, respectively. They helped shaping the field after coming to this conclusion: This is what artificial intelligence is, it performs tasks that, when carried out by human beings, normally require intelligence. What can we infer from this definition? That there are tasks that artificial intelligence performs better than human beings. Or that it produces a certain result in less time than a human being. And AI is delivering a faster result, which is what has happened with LLMs.[3]

Reflecting on this definition, we were able to raise some questions and begin to reimagine what the possibilities might be if we stopped seeing ourselves as mere workers in the AI industry. It's worth noting here – just for clarity – that machine learning is not artificial intelligence in itself; it's a subfield within AI – focused on grouping tastes, people, and thoughts, but artificial intelligence is much broader than that. Machine learning needs to recognize patterns, it needs to work within a standard, you can't start from a blank white sheet. You have to have this defined pattern, and relationships bring me these patterns.

But there are types of pattern learning that aren't normally shared with people, and this can lead to a sense of despair, because they don't allow people to develop strategies to hack[4] these spaces in search of other paths. And there is more than one way of directing the machine learning – but this "learning" is very much in quotation marks. In unsupervised learning, I can have the model training itself, which is a bit like the way LLMs are being built. They need to make these associations based on various links in order to understand what the person is asking or requesting. Whereas in supervised learning I have a bit more control – I can provide a photo, the person's name, and some information about them to the algorithm. So, in a way, I have control over what I want or what I expect the result to be. And then there's what we call reinforcement learning, and this indeed leads us directly into the construction, definition, and development of tools like ChatGPT.

ChatGPT begins to interact with the environment, so in addition to the information it retrieves from the internet and the information we give it, it can look at all the other interactions using sensors. It looks not only at the responses from these interactions but also at our responses, because it needs to mimic the way we write in order to provide its responses, which brings it closer to people emotionally.

ChatGPT tools are directly linked to reinforcement learning.

And there is the understanding that these everyday agents can make decisions by interacting with the environment. They will be either rewarded or penalized. Penalties refer to the people who swear at them – there are lots of people who do that, lots of people who say its responses are wrong, etc. Rewards refer to the people who are going to be polite with the tool and who, in theory, think that this politeness will save them from an apocalypse in the future.

Natural Language and Accessibility

Natural Language Processing (NLP) – a term I don't particularly like, but that is widely used and appears in the main reference works in the field – refers to enabling machines to understand, interpret, and generate natural language. One might ask: but what is natural language? If you ask someone in the field of linguistics: "What is natural language?" or "What is language?," you will realize that the complexity of natural language transcends the simplifications sought by these tools in their attempt to achieve a single model.

For me, this is where one of the dangers of this phase we are living through lies: with the tools used to mimic texts, for example, people are not being educated. Teenagers and children

already growing up with these tools are not being educated to think critically about their feedback, nor to interpret it, because they assume that those texts and that feedback are already true. There is no questioning back. If you ask them what natural language is, they'll say: "Oh, the ChatGPT text says…" The references have changed. And those of us who are working on essay analysis are very concerned about this. Because there is a substitution of references, a substitution of how punctuation occurs in sentences and of sentence construction itself.

There are natural language techniques that are being used without people knowing, based on the information they are sharing on networks. One of them is text summarization. When you ask a specific tool to summarize a large volume of text, pay attention to how the summary opens. And if it's a summary of more than one paragraph, pay attention to the beginnings of each paragraph, so you'll notice a repetition. Summarization is carried out like this: the tool takes the main idea of the first paragraph and replicates it in all the following paragraphs. That's the repetition. When you use any of these tools, pay attention to this summarization.

Another technique widely used in these tools is translation. It has evolved a lot because of accessibility. Today there are several tools that even translate into Libras[5] without the need for an interpreter. The danger I see in this is that sign language changes depending on where you are, so the fact that you try to standardize and homogenize it hinders creativity, since it is still being built, and this harms communication in the deaf community. This is an interesting point to think about: we only look at the translation from one language to another without considering this aspect of accessibility. When we focus on accessibility, there's another context to consider.

And the third widely used technique is emotion analysis, which is a great marketing tool, frequently employed in communication. It became popular with Facebook, then with X.[6] It consists of evaluating the emotional tone of a text, based on the words used and the construction of the sentence. Many people become fearful when they get to this part, but it's not necessarily the emotional tone that the tool is evaluating. You can construct a sentence such as: "I like dogs." It takes "like," which is a verb, and associates it with the definition of like. This action results in a narrowing of the definition of the verb "like," which will establish the tone of the sentence: an emotional, sentimental tone… It's purely logical. The tool looks for the verb in the sentence and, based on the definition of the verb, constructs what it thinks is the final result: liking dogs, liking coffee… And then it presents the outcome: this has a positive tone or this has a delicate tone, giving adjectives that make us believe that it is an analysis of feeling, an emotional analysis.

Ethics

The area I work in is computer vision. Ethics and computer vision is an area that also began during World War II, but became a little more popular in the 1980s, when there was an increase not only in economic power but also in the number of hardware products developed that could process images and videos at much greater speed.

When I started in this area, I did a lot of work with emotion recognition. You laugh, I go there, capture that smile and create an emoji, for example. This type of technique was used in the evolution of facial recognition, which is within the field of computer vision.

Facial recognition detects what is most important in the face. So, if my algorithm detects that the nose, the mouth, and the eyes are the most important features, then cheeks, wrinkles, and eyebrows will be excluded. Because what I have detected as most important to build the face is the mouth, the nose, and the eyes. So this detection fails because it doesn't take in all the information about the face.

In the case of facial recognition, detection is often done using the iris of our eyes. Everyone must have seen a news story about people selling their irises in São Paulo for 600 reais.[7] The iris is unique, so if you do facial recognition using iris detection, you can be sure that the person is that person. And if you take the iris and cross-reference it with other information, you'll find that person's context. That's the problem with selling the iris: all the information that is attached to it.

And then concepts are built from there. What are these concepts? I reproduce this image of the parts of a person's face in another area of the machine, in the algorithm, and I go on reconstructing it and combining parts until I reconstruct that person's face. This happens a lot in the search for missing persons. But this same technique has been used for facial recognition. People often put facial recognition down to images – in other words, they think that if there are more images of Black people, it will work. But that's not quite true.

By definition, facial recognition is a dangerous tool. Because the fact that you use someone's physical characteristics to make a decision about their life is dangerous in itself. In my case, I study object recognition, the ethics behind it, and the conclusion is that there are no ethics involved in these tools.

Education as Technology

Investing time in planning, in lesson plans, which are often not monitored by the school itself, is something that teachers have always complained about. This monitoring, helping the teachers, guiding them, for example, is one of the responsibilities of the pedagogical coordinator. They take the teachers' lesson plans and attempt to ensure that they survive all the difficulties of day-to-day life in the classroom. But often, teachers set this plan aside, because the difficulties are greater than the lesson plan, and there is no follow-up on this work.

There is no incentive in this regard. There is no discussion about how this plan should be drawn up and what the expectation for it is. Because planning has always been a point of discussion, both during strikes and at teachers' meetings. I come from a family of teachers, so I've heard this all my life.

Do you want to use artificial intelligence and force it on the teachers and students in the classroom? Then let's hack that and turn it into something else: let's force schools to change the structures of the lesson plan. For this to happen, people need to understand these AI concepts, not to distance themselves from it, but to try to get closer. It's hard to imagine other uses for ChatGPT, for example, because what has been presented to us is a structure.

During the pandemic, the teaching staff were responsible for the class's WhatsApp group with parents and students. And at the same time as they were teaching, they had to record the audio to pass on to students who didn't have access to the internet. These teachers work in areas where it's more difficult to hold the discussions we're having here, for example. And there is the issue that, in order to discuss this aspect of support, there is a whole layer of access to networks, to technology, to the organization of information, from which many people are still excluded.

The role of the educational field is to bring about this critical thinking. The educational field is not responsible for providing, for example, access to the internet or networks. It doesn't even have the capacity to do so, considering the way we are structured in Brazil.

So that's it: logistical challenges, network access challenges… How much does the educational field contribute to breaking down these paradigms that technology merely updates and to which it offers no alternatives? It's often nice to visualize this reinforcement of critical thinking within the field, and to do it in different formats. Another point – which became very clear during the pandemic – is the need/importance for educators not to beat themselves up for not being able to carry out activities that are beyond the scope of the field in which they are working. This is a dynamic that we explore when we bring in more emotional aspects – in other words, the emotional impact that constant criticism can have on people. I think it's important to look beyond mere criticism, you know? Turning criticism into reality, into action.

1   In 1942, before the term "artificial intelligence" was coined, the British mathematician Alan Turing (1912–1954) developed Bombe, an electromechanical machine for deciphering German messages encrypted by another machine, the Enigma. It wasn't until 1956 that American computer scientist John McCarthy (1927–2011) coined the term "artificial intelligence" during the Dartmouth Conference, widely regarded as the foundational milestone of the field.

2   The term "cluster" in the context of marketing refers to a strategy for segmenting the target audience into groups with common characteristics in order to optimize a company's results.

3   LLMs (Large Language Models) are artificial intelligence models trained with vast data from the internet in order to understand and generate text. Popularized by ChatGPT, they learn patterns in the use of words and phrases, so when they are given an input, they predict the most likely continuation.

4   The term "hacking," in this context, is used in a broader sense of creative subversion of systems or expectations, going beyond its origins in the field of computing.

5   Libras is the acronym for Brazilian Sign Language, officially recognized since 2002 as the language used by deaf communities in Brazil.

6   The social network formerly known as Twitter.

7   In Brazil, the General Data Protection Law (LGPD) considers irises to be highly sensitive personal data. Unlike fingerprints, which can fail or be replicated, irises offer the most accurate and secure form of human identification. At the beginning of 2025, cases of people in São Paulo agreeing to have their irises scanned in exchange for cryptocurrency sparked debate on social media and in the National Congress.

Conversation with T-Michael

Bonaventure Soh Bejeng Ndikung

Conversation held in April, 2025.

Bonaventure Soh Bejeng Ndikung: Good afternoon. And welcome to this last day of the fourth *Invocation* for the 36th edition of the Bienal de São Paulo. It's a great pleasure to see you all. I would like to start with a word of thanks. As usual, when we come into a space, we give thanks to the people that hold the space.

Professor Kenji, thank you for your hospitality. Thank you for giving us this space. I think it deserves a round of applause, please. Many thanks to Andrew Maerkle for your very moving words. It was deeply touching, really personally. We do these things because they matter to us. We're not doing it for art's sake. We're doing it for humanity's sake, for society's sake. Thank you for touching on these incredible life stories. Thanks also to Kanako Sugiyama and all those that have been involved in the preparation of these *Invocations*. The many people in the background that make this possible. Tomoya Iwata, and many others. And the team in São Paulo that is supporting us from afar. And thank you, Arai, for the wonderful poems that you just read.

It was a beautiful weaving from the loom to talking about garments, talking about design, talking about fashion, talking about art. And I am particularly pleased to have this conversation with somebody that I consider one of the greatest artists of our time. A shapeshifter.

Somebody with an incredible sense of beauty. I don't know who was talking about that recently. But a few weeks ago, I was in Paris with [curator and writer] Simon Njami. And I asked him, What are you working on these days? He said he was writing about beauty. And he said that is one of the most radical things to do in our time. I think that's what you've been doing for a very long time, T-Michael. So it's a great pleasure to be with you.

I will start by reading a kind of an introduction to T. Michael. A short biography. When I asked him to send me a short biography, he sent me five versions. One very short one. Another one labeled "Art Speak." Another one, a longer version, and so on and so forth. So I chose the long version, because you need to understand what people do if you have to listen to them talk. So I will read that out to you and then ask questions after that.

We will ramble through things. It's also important to say that this conversation we're going to have today could have been a conversation in a bar. So just think of yourselves as people around a table in a bar, participating or listening to us talk. So the extended version goes as such.

T-Michael is a Ghanaian-Norwegian bespoke tailor, designer, and multidisciplinary artist based in Bergen, Norway. With over 29 years of experience, he is known for his conceptual approach to tailoring, blending traditional craftsmanship with modern aesthetics. His work spans multiple creative ventures, including T-Michael, his eponymous label that focuses on tailoring and menswear with a distinct innovative touch; Norwegian Rain, a high-end outerwear brand that combines sartorial elegance with technical functionality, specializing in stylish waterproof garments; T. Kimono, a contemporary take on the classic Japanese kimono, merging tradition with modern silhouettes and craftsmanship; Film Lab, a platform for producing short films that reflect his artistic vision and storytelling, and T. Creative Spaces, a hub for exploring and fostering creativity across various disciplines.

T-Michael's work is deeply rooted in sartorial traditions, yet he consistently challenges norms and redefines tailoring with a cultural and artistic narrative. His meticulous attention to detail and commitment to impeccable construction set his designs apart, making him a distinctive force in contemporary fashion and design. I chose to read this version of his biography because it sounded to me like poetry. The other ones were too banal.

This one is befitting of him. So, thank you, T-Michael, for accepting our invitation.

T-Michael: Thank you for inviting me. It's a pleasure.

BSBN: I have prepared a few questions and we will try to follow them. We will definitely go offline, and that's fine. And the first one was, I would like you to begin by touching on your biography, you know, with something I would like to call the cartographic biography. A biography that maps and connects Ghana to the UK to Norway to Japan and other places. How does T. Michael weave these different geographies together?

T-M: Good evening. It's nice to see so many beautiful people here. And I hope we can have a great conversation together. And I hope we can touch each other somehow. And we all leave here feeling a little more refreshed than when we came in. Now, to the question. I normally tell people I'm on my way to the North Pole. I was born in Ghana.

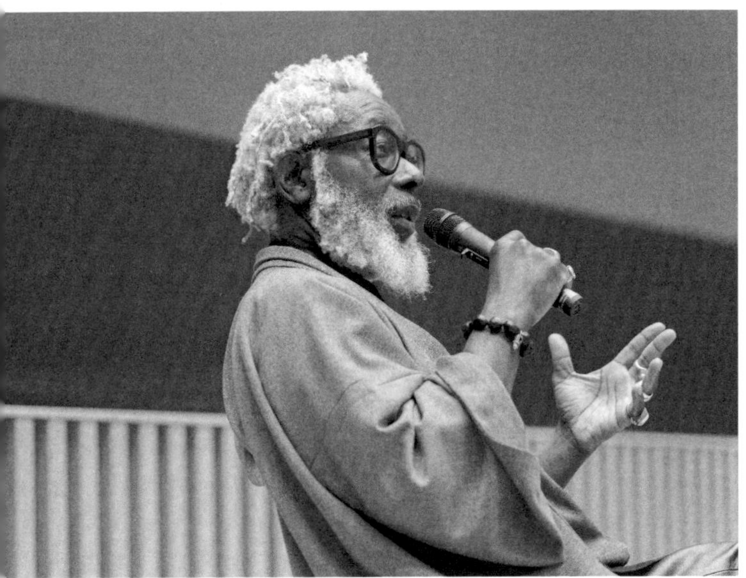

Moved to London. Spent my formative years there. Then I moved to Norway. Love took me to Norway. I fell in love with this beautiful woman, she was Norwegian, so after a while we lived in London, she decided to move back to Norway.

And we thought we'd give it a go, so we went to Norway. And I think, in hindsight, I would say that moving to Norway practically formed the way I look at everything these days. The fact that I'm leaving in third place from Ghana through London to Norway gives me the ability to be able to distance myself from what is around me and have a different kind of gaze on it. And this gaze, it's a gift, I would say, because sometimes you get muddled up in things.

BSBN: Take us to some other place with that. It is said that our primary skin or home is our body. And the secondary is what we wear. The tertiary, our apartment, our house, and the rest follows. In one of Bella Freud's Fashion Neurosis series with Eric Cantona, the football star, he talks about the importance of feeling good in one's body. I mentioned that earlier today.

In French, you respond to the question, "comment tu te portes, comment as-tu," by saying, "je me porte bien." I carry myself well. I wanted you to talk about this negotiation between the primary space, the primary skin, and the secondary. How

135

does one get to that point of, "je me porte bien," with garments, with fabrics?

T-M: From a creator's point of view, I like to think that we create based on our skill set and our foresight. We create garments cut right that will give you that support. This is mathematical. There are numbers, there are calculations. Even if the garment will be loose, it's cut right, it will sit on you and give you that support. It will brace you well. That lifts you up and gives you that air of feeling good in your body. That's the first part of it. The moment you get that, it's easier to transform that into your thoughts and be able to present yourself in good ways in front of other people.

I think dressing well, in any form you take it, shows how you respect the people around you. I think if someone invites you over to dinner and they spend all night cooking something great, you want to show up at least looking a little bit decent. This, for me, is also part of why I do what I do.

It gives me the opportunity to be able to reflect and mirror my thoughts in my clothing. I love tradition. I think tradition sets the course for everything we do. But at the same time, if we're not challenging tradition, if we're not trying to change things, then practically things just freeze and slow down. Tradition itself will just dissolve, because it's not exciting for anyone to do anymore. They become redundant.

The fact is, we need to shake things up. We need to create this space where tradition can be challenged. Over time, that will keep it going because it reflects a little bit of the contemporary. Over time, that will crystallize into, for the next generation, what tradition is supposed to be.

BSBN: There is this misunderstanding that tradition is something in the past. While tradition exists, tradition has always been present. It should be dynamic. I think the practice of thinking with tradition, beyond the dichotomy of tradition versus modern, whatever that means, is thinking in continuity. We all come from somewhere. We all have to situate ourselves within particular spaces and histories.

I think, yes, tradition cannot be in the past. It cannot be behind us. Actually, it's ahead of us. For every fashion designer, the moment of presentation of one's collection on the catwalk or in a showroom is one of the most important moments. In my free time, I like to watch these presentations of many of your colleagues.

I can't help to think that walking through the markets of Bamenda, of Yaoundé, of Kumasi, or Accra, I often see more inspiring and sophisticated and better crafted garments than on the catwalks of Paris or London or New York. I understand that we do not need to think of these binaries. I would like for you to paint for us an image of the streets and markets of Accra or Kumasi or some of these places and how they might possibly impact your work.

T-M: I should comment on the fact that catwalks are a product of capitalism. They are created not just for the show itself but to sell clothing. They are very, very calculated.

On the streets and the market in Accra, Kumasi, or wherever you go, this is something else. This is self-expression. People are walking out there with what may seem so much – or either so much or very little – but in that little space of time, they are carrying on themselves what they believe is the best representation of themselves for that day. There's an air of presence. There's an air of satisfaction. They are selling things that I love to see on the streets everywhere I go.

It's how people put their clothes together, because we are very different. The way people put their clothes together will tell a little bit about, maybe, the society they live in, where they come from, and so on and so forth. In a way, what I look for is to see all the things that I'm thinking are ill-fitting, because for me that is what fashion is. Anything that doesn't fit in is what, for me, is right. You see, I'm very much interested in those who dare not to fit in.

> **BSBN:** One of the few reasons I went to church on Sundays was to see the catwalk. I think the people went to church for that, to present themselves.

T-M: They still do.

> **BSBN:** Of course, to present themselves to some God, but also to each other. The way these women would wrap the fabrics around them, the headscarf, the details, the earrings, the rings, and so on and so forth. It was as every person was like a piece of art put together. I'm interested in that. Sometimes, I look at designers and I miss all that. I miss all those darings, to dare clash colors, forms, concepts of beauty.

T-M: The problem is where people are chasing the bread, others are chasing the money. When you have big businesses owning practically everything, it means every time they need to make so much money to keep it going. Yes, you have a few designers that will shake up the establishment and create brilliant things, but that's not where you go to find inspiration. Inspiration is the people that are running independent setups, people that are wearing their hats on their sleeves, people that are super creative and would not try and fit in. Again, I keep saying this. First of all, you need to attain the knowledge. You need to understand the foundation of what you're doing, because knowledge gives you the opportunity to be able to mess things up. The moment you understand how something works, it's easier to play with it. First of all, a great foundation.

BSBN: Is that why you surround yourself with other creative people, other artists? I see a lot of musicians, painters, sculptors in your universe. Absolutely.

T-M: From what I'm saying, I think you probably understand that clothing or fashion is not where I go for inspiration. I actually don't really follow any fashion at all. I'm more interested in creative people.

Like you said, musicians, sculptors, ceramicists, anything that is created from someone's mind through their hands, from the heart to the hand, that's what inspires me. Because when I go to someone else's show or their exhibition and I get inspired, I want to run back home and create something beautiful because that's where the magic lies. Someone can come to my space and have this glow around their face, something that is very difficult to get, but when you manage it, that's the satisfaction.

So, the Nigerian-American artist… Calm down, breathe. Now go and see someone else's work. The moment you've seen it, it will give you this urgency to create something that is also powerful. This is what inspires me. People are people everywhere you go. If you tap into the people's angle, everything just opens up like a flower. That's where the magic lies.

BSBN: So, we have to slowly come to an end, and I think it would be unfair for me to finish this conversation without asking the critical question in the room, which is, as beautiful as some of these suits, these t-kimonos, these shirts and trousers you make are, they're damn expensive. So, the question is, how can we actually afford for a t-michael? I'm asking this question in relation also to sustainability.

T-M: Yes, that's a beautiful question. That's actually a very beautiful question because the thing is, when products are well made, they do tend to cost a little bit more. It takes time to develop these ideas.

138

It takes time to get these right fabrics. The fabrics are well made. The whole technology behind it, we talked about it already. It is made to last. As much as I make clothing, I'm not really interested in people shopping from me. I want them to get a piece, and I want them to use this piece as long as they can until it falls apart. And then they may patch it too. There is a certain amount of... I look at it as an art form.

It's not about buying one jacket on the weekend, and then picking up another one the next weekend, and then a third one on week after that. It's about finding that piece that works for you, and really wearing it your way. If I meet you on the street, and I see the way that suits you, that will suit me, then I think I've done my job right.

BSBN: How do we conjugate humanity, Michael?

T-M: By waking up every morning and thinking, how does the world go round? The world goes round by thinking that everyone should be linked to you somehow. Any business, no matter what you do, is always about people. The more you engage with people, the better you have a chance at succeeding at what you do. That, for me, is the basis of any form of conjugating humanity. Thank you very much. Thank you.

Upcycling: An Affective and Political Technology

Manauara Clandestina

Text developed from an online conversation between the Fundação Bienal team and the artist Manauara Clandestina, held on April 10, 2025.

Upcycling

Upcycling was a revelation for me because I came from a background where fashion was synonymous with big brands and expensive items. Upcycling revealed itself to be a technology of possibility and a way of life because it is nothing more than taking old, discarded, or unwanted items and transforming them into new products with new looks and concepts.

We have been spreading the word. I transform what has been left behind, renewing notions of what something once was. So, I analyze the bodies of transvestites and cis Black women, which often become abject in the context of everyday racism. I see upcycling as a way of dealing with a body that is, in a way, socially neglected.

For me, working with upcycling is a challenge that helps me realize the connections it brings. It is not just a way of dressing up. It is how I make films today: a patchwork of emotional memories recorded with clips from old footage that I find relevant. I take this thread and weave it together. This approach is not limited to clothing; upcycling extends to the way I think and deal with things in my daily life.

Belonging

I say that church was my fine arts school because that is where it all began. When there was no more room for me there, I realized I had to spread my wings – life has always been like that in my mind. I had always dreamed about it. When I was very young, I used to tell my brothers that one day I would leave and live by myself in São Paulo. Then I grew up and left. I am living out the dreams I had as a child.

Eager to belong to something – to this trend, to this community that does not belong to me but to rich people – I was welcomed by upcycling. I confess that when I first looked at it, I thought: "What is this? Is this fashion? Fashion is Chanel; fashion is Louis Vuitton." But when I started to see myself in it, I realized that that is the way society treats us. Society does not want to look at the transvestite's face. Society does not want to know what happened. It only wants to see beauty – if even that.

It is almost like self-analysis. I am doing this because I love this practice, but, more importantly, because I see myself in it. When I accepted that my art would be based on trash, I also embraced my poor childhood in the church with the prayer circle sisters and my mother. I'm recreating an emotional cycle, but this time it's just me, in my own space, my territory. It is no longer within a Christian territory, in the church and all that, but I am still my mother's daughter.

Affective Crossroads

I would describe my work as collective. When I met Vicenta Perrotta[1] and the studio, I was in a vulnerable situation, caught between living on the streets and staying in a shelter. Then I was embraced by sewing. And I realized that I had also been given a mission of affection in the studio. I made a point of ensuring that my work would not be solitary. Of course, this is not always possible, but it is the foundation of my practice. My work would not exist if not for this affective crossroads because that is how things are built. There is no way to create *Migranta*,[2] for instance, by talking about a solo immigration experience. Not least because I was not the only transvestite treated that way at the Barcelona airport. After some time living there, I met other Brazilian trans women, who told me that they had experienced the same situation at the airport. In other words, they intimidate you so that you enter the city afraid. It's a policy that instills fear. During my first days in the city, I trembled when I saw the police, just as I did in Brazil. Without this collective affection, I might not have been mentally strong enough to talk about this crossing experience.

I cannot create a theory about upcycling on my own because it is part of a collective political mindset. You have to spend time with these people and show them that upcycling is possible. Sometimes, the clothes might not turn out so well. However, spending time together in the studio and having conversations were important for us to bond. Like my parents, who are missionaries, I have a mission. They take the Bible, and perhaps I take upcycling. It is a way for me to connect with the girls. Photography is too. Upcycling has undoubtedly brought me together with people who hustle and have something to do with my work or my resilience in the world. I find parts of myself in these people and these processes.

Fashion, Consumption, and Behavior

Fashion is an anthropological study of behavior in itself. I have loved fashion since I was a child and have always been interested in it, even in a small town in the state of Amazonas. Whenever I could, I tuned in. Now that I am an adult working as an artist, I realize that I cannot agree with fashion that creates trends hostile to nature and the environment. It is a racist agenda because it places fashion in a position of an unattainable status. I did not see myself as someone who would follow that way of thinking and consume that fashion. So I have been following a path toward upcycling because it makes sense to me as a cross-dresser. It is amazing how you can tell who a person is by the way they dress. I am not talking about brands or anything like that. It is about how they behave in relation to that consumption or how they present themselves to the world. Upcycling has undoubtedly made me think a lot about this because it does not usually carry the same symbols as mainstream fashion.

All of this is undoubtedly linked to my identity as well. When you identify a cross-dresser, it is usually not just because of their gender; it is also because of how they dress and behave. I am reflecting on this. The path toward finding a sense of belonging undoubtedly goes through clothing. With this technology, you think about consumption and the environment. It has to do with your body and what you experience in your daily life. I have tried not to neglect these intersections anymore because they are a part of me and my daily life. They are generated by the way I dress and behave with fashion.

Unfamiliarity

Upcycling generates a sense of unfamiliarity because it does not conform to a common mold of what people would wear. It still makes cisgender white people, who grew up with this idea of white, unsustainable fashion, feel really uncomfortable. It makes them unhappy to see that now we, transvestites from the margins, are bringing "trash" to these places in a way that can no longer be ignored. Because these people created these territories precisely so that we would not inhabit them, and we have arrived to challenge this. It is a very positive development. In fact, there is tension when you arrive in a space of fashion and art, and people realize that you work with trash.

In the begining, we heard harsh criticisms from people who had no idea what we were doing, and sometimes even our models were barred from entering an event. We blazed this trail through sheer determination. While fashion designers received funding to do their work – and ordinary work, what had always been done – we never had any support for working with trash. It wasn't pleasing to their eyes. And it should have been the complete opposite. They should have understood that we were introducing a new technology, a novelty, and embraced it. But it is not how it was at first. It took patience to understand that this was just the beginning and that things would move forward at some point.

Today, there are other transvestites and stylists who are doing this, including bringing fashion to their neighborhoods. And now, thanks to textile transmutation, they are being taken to workshops and educational institutions. For me, it is already a wonderful outcome to realize that we will not remain silent. And our movement is ancestral. We want people to rethink what they are doing, and consumption and waste too, and how we relate to it. We want them to rethink what they think is disposable.

Technology

Technology is about resignifying waste. For me, that is the greatest effect of upcycling, which is when you no longer neglect waste. Because we think: "I throw this away and it disappears from my sight." But when we see trash as a possibility, it gives new meaning to many things. It has huge benefits for the environment, but it also undoubtedly changes behaviors in relation to consumption, to this policy that pretends there is no environmental collapse in textile production in the world today. Upcycling is a life skill, because it gives you a new way of thinking about your body, what you wear, and how you present yourself to the world, but above all, it allows you to make a personal commitment to the territory and the world in which you live. This practice is even therapeutic for me, as a transvestite, in dealing with this neglect of the trans population, the black population. I realize that there is immense power in this technology and that it is rejected precisely because it does not have this pact of consumption, this pact that fashion has, this thing of the inaccessible or of what is for the few. It is as if fashion and these fine things were distant from our reality, when, in fact, what we need to think about is: is this really what I want to consume for my future?

Migranta

Migranta (2021) came about after my first artist residency in London, my first outside Brazil, which was at the Delfina Foundation. There was already something on my mind that was really getting to me, which was the clothing worn by construction workers. This had started here in São Paulo. Somehow, this aesthetic had always attracted me. And I began to understand, comprehend, relate, in some way, to these men. Initially, back then, still as a prostitute, and later as an artist, I realized that it was like immigration attire. That the men who were working in these clothes were not from the city where I was. They were all migrants from the state of São Paulo, from the Northeast and the North. And, in the case of London, from Eastern Europe.

When my residency in London ended, I put my foot down and said I wasn't going back to Brazil. I wanted to make a film about it. In my mind, I was going to make an upcycling fashion film that would bring together research on the clothing of workers and immigrants. But then I was badly treated at Barcelona airport and spent several hours being interrogated, facing a horrible situation. I talk about this in the film. *Migranta* is, in fact, revenge against the way I was treated at the airport. What was supposed to be a fashion film also became a political manifesto. As time went by, I came to this decision and gained strength, because it was a collective of Latin American people who were part of this work that made Migranta a family project, a real quilombo. I filmed *Migranta* with my scholarship money. It wasn't an easy budget. Especially because I wouldn't have been able to pay everyone who actually worked with me there. And they worked in the middle of the pandemic. *Migranta* has a lot of power from this revenge and from understanding my hatred. Because I still have a lot of hatred. *Migranta* was one of the ways in which I perhaps organized this hatred. And also this beauty, because I didn't stop upcycling. Upcycling, in fact, was the link for people to come, bring things, and sew.

Migranta gives me great hope because it is not just a film; it has become a movement, even though I left Barcelona, a vogue house there in Barcelona, run by a family of Latin artists. *Migranta* has also become a performance collective of Latin artists who are working in

Europe and performing. In a way, we left a legacy for the city. It's something I like to ask myself: what can a group of organized transvestites do? We took that hatred as fuel and kept going.

8. Future

I am the future. I live in the future. I am in the future. I am discussing a strategy for the present. For me, the present is already the future. I have lived many lives in this one already. So, I converse with the future. The future could not exist without Xica Manicongo. It could not exist without my mother and the ladies from the church, who collected old furniture from the streets and, together, in a workshop, refurbished them and distributed them among themselves. Transvestites and black people already have these technologies for this future. We are deprived of this future, but we live this future now. And I am in a future of organized transvestites. And this time, they will not stop until they are heard and seen. I live in a future where my ancestors had to suffer greatly for me to be here. The idea of the future, for me, is to move and dress myself, to adorn myself with what was improperly thrown away, with what was left behind. My idea of the future is to understand that I am also a possibility. That I am not limited to a street corner or the night. I am that future. I am also the future of this generation that is rethinking the way it behaves in relation to life, to art. The future is now. I can't think that the future would be, I don't know, 2040. We are in 2025, folks. We are living that future now, without a doubt.

1   Vicenta Perrotta, an artist and fashion designer born in Campinas (SP) in 1979, works with recycled materials, primarily textile waste, to create garments centered on the concept of textile transmutation, which she herself developed. In 2013, she founded Ateliê TRANSmoras, a space that offers training in cutting and sewing for the trans community, promoting income generation and autonomy. Perrota describes herself an artist who uses fashion to tell stories and bring about transformation through inclusive fashion shows, with performances and makeup designed for trans bodies. For more information, see: https://revistacontinente.com.br/edicoes/247/vicenta-perrotta--ativismo--moda-e-autonomia-rtransr. Accessed in June 2025.

2   The work, presented at the 60th Venice Biennale – *Foreigners Everywhere* (2024), explores clothing as one of the traces of the passage and escape from coloniality, as well as portraying a personal experience of the artist at Barcelona airport in 2021.

147

Daughter's Daughter

Asako Iwama

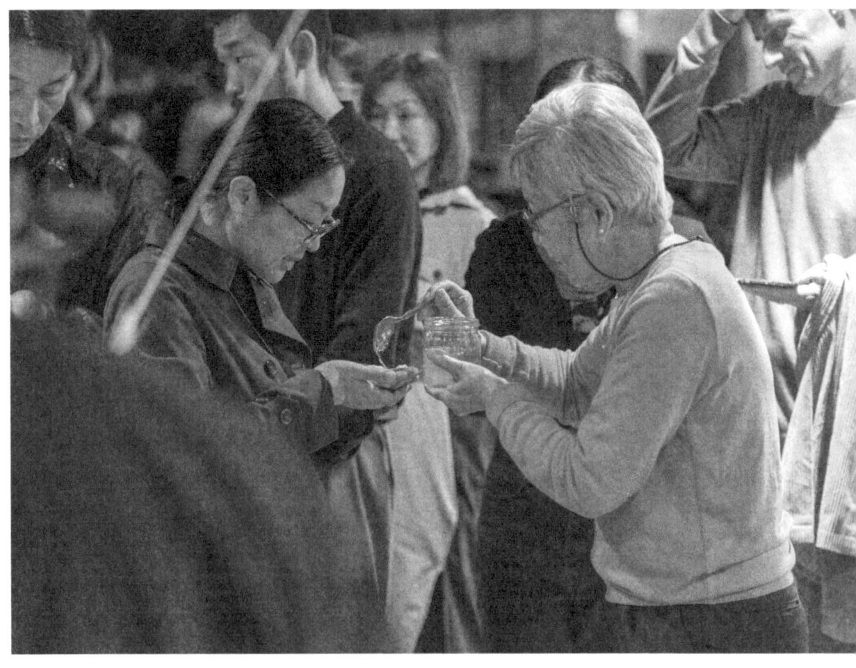

© Naoki Takehisa / Fundação Bienal de São Paulo

Honey [...] is a sort of saliva of the stars,
or the moisture of the air.
– Pliny the Elder, Roman naturalist, 1st century AD

This past winter in Berlin, all of our honeybees died. They were infected with Deformed Wing Virus (DWV), spread by the parasitic Varroa mite. The virus deforms the bees' wings and impairs their cognitive functions.

Each hive holds around ten thousand bees. This winter, they all vanished, as if they had evaporated into thin air.

The honeybee (*Apis mellifera*) is a social insect – communal, efficient, non-individualistic. The structure of the beehive is often compared to a totalitarian state. A single worker bee may fly out up to a thousand times a day to collect nectar. She works for a month, then dies. Every worker bee is a daughter of the queen.

The male bees, or "drones," have the largest eyes. That's right, they are known by the same word used to refer to the unmanned aircrafts developed by corporations like the Israeli defense contractor Elbit Systems. Such aircrafts emit a constant, low-pitched hum when in flight – a sound that can feel unnerving. The term "drone" was inspired by Queen Bee, a pilotless target aircraft produced by the British Navy in 1935.

Today, the sons of the British Empire are using drone technology to kill in Palestine, a land they once colonized.

This honey [here] was made by our bees from spring through summer of last year, before the virus took hold. They labored nonstop. Fanning their wings, they thickened the nectar in the summer heat.

This is the taste of life now gone. Yes, the honey in your kitchen was produced by bees that no longer exist.

149

In November 2024, the German Bundestag [Parliament] passed a resolution against antisemitism, which in turn intensified attacks on those who argue that the Israeli state is a racial apartheid project or support the BDS (Boycott, Divestment, Sanctions) movement. Back in 2019, the Bundestag had already declared that support for BDS is antisemitism, urging institutions to deny funding and venues to anyone who backed the boycott.

Today, as part of its *Staatsräson*, or "reason of state," Germany unconditionally supports Israel, and any criticism of the Israeli government is peremptorily dealt with as antisemitism. The German people remain silent.

Anyone who protests the massacres being committed by the Israeli military in Gaza, opposes illegal settlements in the West Bank, or expresses solidarity with Palestine is branded an "antisemite"– even when they are themselves Jewish. The Jewish critics of Israel's policies are called "bad Jews." It is as if Germany – the very nation that orchestrated the Holocaust and murdered six million Jews – now claims the right to decide who is a "good Jew" or not.

***

In 2022 I took a beekeeping course. There, I met a different kind of person: mostly older men, retired, and some about my age, sipping Coca-Cola from plastic bottles. Their concern was not pesticides, nor privatized water, nor microplastics, but honey yield. To them, bees are livestock.

Zyklon B, originally a pesticide, was employed by Nazi Germany beginning in 1942. Tens of thousands of tons were used at Auschwitz-Birkenau alone, where 1.1 million people were murdered. I visited Auschwitz for the first time in March. Brick chimneys stand out among the ruins. The buildings had been destroyed to erase evidence. But the chimneys remain, still pointing skyward.

Bayer, the German pharmaceutical and chemical giant, was once part of IG Farben, which produced Zyklon B. In the 1940s Monsanto supplied Saccharin to Coca-Cola. Later, Monsanto developed Roundup (glyphosate) and genetically modified soy and corn seeds. In 2018 Bayer acquired Monsanto. After October 7, 2023, Bayer raised the Israeli flag over its Berlin headquarters.

Bayer is also a major producer of the neonicotinoid pesticides, including imidacloprid and clothianidin, blamed for the mass die-off of honeybees. In 2006 there were reports of colony collapse disorder (CCD) in the US. The phenomenon is linked to the neurotoxicity of these pesticides, which disorient bees and prevent them from returning to their hives.

150

***

In 2023, after completing my training, I bought two queen bees and their daughters from a beekeeper by a lake in Berlin.

Forager bees collect nectar from flowers using their proboscis, store it in their honey sacs, and pass it from mouth to mouth to waiting worker bees upon returning to the hive. The worker bees then evaporate the moisture in the nectar by fanning their wings. Enzymes in the bees' saliva break down the nectar's sucrose into glucose and fructose. When the moisture content reaches 20%, the worker bees seal it with wax. The result – 80% sugar – is nearly imperishable.

According to the United Nation's Food and Agriculture Organization, bees pollinate over a third of global crops. But with habitat destruction, infections, and climate change, pollinator insects are disappearing – to be replaced by artificial pollination. This shift will have a profound impact on global food supply.

***

Germany's silence suffocates its immigrants. After October 7, 2023, the mask fell. The country's *Erinnerungskultur* – "memory culture" – proved hollow. The idea was that the German people would confront the crimes of the Nazis and speak about them openly. They would cultivate their imagination to ensure that the mistakes of the past never happened again. But what, truly, have we learned over these eighty years?

When tens of thousands gathered at the Brandenburg Gate to protest the rise of the far right, they did not see the Islamophobia and Arabophobia within themselves. They speak out against fascism at home, yet fall silent before apartheid and colonialism in Palestine.

In March workers at Berlin's public transport company BVG went on strike for better wages and conditions. Meanwhile, Germany and the European Union expanded their military budgets, seeking to stimulate the economy through war while ignoring its toll on lives and the planet.

***

If Rosa Luxemburg – the Polish-born, Jewish revolutionary – had succeeded in her democratic, anti-imperialist revolution of 1919, the Holocaust might never have happened.

In a letter from 1898, sent shortly after she moved to Berlin, Rosa wrote of the city:

> Cold, tasteless, massive – a real barracks; and the dear Prussians with their arrogance, as though every one of them had swallowed the stick with which they had once been beaten.

More than a century later, Berlin feels the same. The atmosphere in 2025 feels like Rosa's time again – a police state surrounded by the far-right AfD. The very "stick" Rosa spoke of – Germany has swallowed once more. Today, the police wield that stick against protesters who denounce the genocide of the Palestinians. Those who remain silent seem to stand as if their spines were fused with that stick.

Rosa Luxemburg opposed World War I, struggled for the emancipation of the workers, and co-led the Spartacus League, a radical socialist group and precursor to the German Communist Party, with fellow socialist Karl Liebknecht. In 1919, after a failed uprising, Rosa and Karl were arrested. Karl was bludgeoned and shot. Rosa was beaten, shot in the head, and thrown into a canal – her body missing for months.

In 1926, architect Ludwig Mies van der Rohe built a brick monument in their honor. He said, "As [they] were shot in front of a brick wall, a brick wall would be what I would build as a monument."[1]

In 1935, the Nazis destroyed the monument. Rosa's writings were burned.

Rosa's name lives on – as a subway station on Berlin's U2 line, as a street name, and as a small square in front of the Volksbühne theater.

***

Why couldn't Germany stop the Holocaust? Because of silence – because "we didn't know." And now it is happening all over again.

Every morning I walk down Torstrasse with my child to the bus stop by Rosa-Luxemburg-Straße. Every day we walk toward her name – the woman who stood with the working class, who opposed war and was brutally executed on January 15, 1919.

As we near the intersection, my child spots hand-sized stickers on the walls and poles. "Look, Mama, there's one," he points out. "Free Palestine."

Even at seven, he knows that to say the word "Palestine" in Germany means choosing the moment carefully. Finding a sticker feels like a treasure. "There it is!" he whispers with excitement.

The stickers depict watermelons, Palestinian flags[2] – signs of solidarity.

***

Let the saliva of bees who no longer exist drip onto these baked bricks. Take what was never voiced, grind it like grains of rye, mix it with your own saliva – and swallow.

1   Mies ven der Rohe, apud Nathaniel Flakin, *Revolutionary Berlin: A Walking Guide*. London: Pluto Press, 2022, 67.

2   The watermelon has been used as a symbol of Palestine because, when cut open, the fruit displays the same colors as the Palestinian national flag: red, black, white and green. See "How the Watermelon Became a Symbol of Palestinian Solidarity," Time, Oct. 20, 2023. Available at https://time.com/6326312/watermelon-palestinian-symbol-solidarity. Accessed in May, 2025.

Ancestral Technology: Oral Traditions, Memory, and Spirituality

Gê Viana

Text developed from an online conversation held on April 10, 2025, between the Fundação Bienal and the artist Gê Viana.

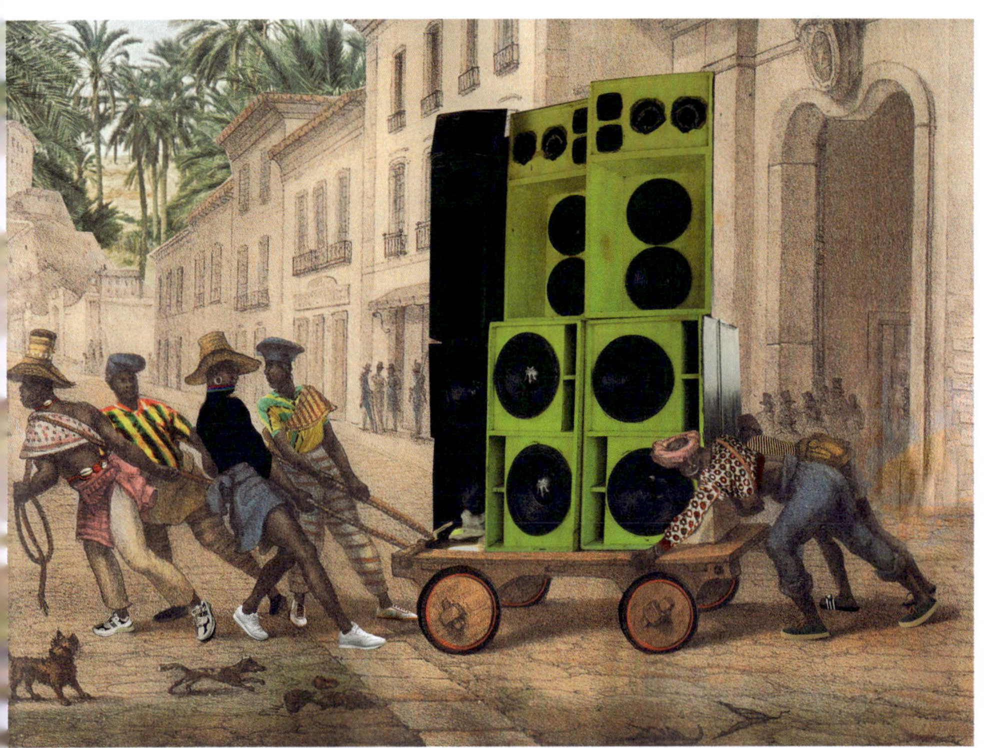

Gê Viana
Radiola de Promessa [Radiola of Promise], 2022
From the series **Atualizações de Rugendas** [Rugendas Update]
Cutout and collage on paper, 33,5 × 27 cm

Prelude

This is my first work[1] that does not draw on colonial archives. It's a crazy Invocation that I was given. And I thought: how am I going to develop this? What would be another way of looking at these archives, of interacting with my own archive, one that I have fabulated over so many years? When Thiago [de Paula Souza] proposed that I not use these images, which he calls "ghosts," he ended up pushing me off an already very comfortable axis. Because nowadays we know that there is a very frequent practice of collage and photomontage based on the historical images made by the travelers who arrived in Brazil in the colonial period, whom I like to call "visajantes," which is like a traveling visage.

And then, when I started collecting the images made by these travelers, it was a bit challenging to produce *Atualizações traumáticas de Debret*[2] [Traumatic Updates of Debret], because the series is based on these paintings made by travelers from the colonial period which depict a very precarious way of life when portraying this population. In my collage practice, there is this attention to details, there is the creation of clothing, and one thing you see in most of the lithographs made by these men is that people are often facing downwards. So, in my collages, I try to raise that face. We cannot see the eyes of these people, these people aren't depicted with their eyes alive in these lithographs, in these watercolors, so what I do is a sketch of what an ancient ancestor might look like.

I started producing the series *Atualizações traumáticas de Debret*, but then I put it aside, because it was no longer about Debret, it was *Radiola de promessa* [Radiola of Promise]. These original *quilombola*[3] people who appear in my collages… It's no longer Debret's work, it's our collage, it's our history, it's also appropriating our own authorship, which no longer needs to be linked to those travelers. This new work that I'm presenting at the Bienal reflects a moment in my life that allows me to portray and give a leading role to these people. Obviously, it's important to think of this archive as something we can appropriate and reflect on outside the colonial narrative. This is something I've been examining a lot in my work.

Our ancestors never stopped celebrating, cheering, and rejoicing. So why isn't this presented to us within this narrative? That was the trigger for me to start using these images. And I think that's where the resistance lies, you know? It lies in assimilating life in a beautiful way, in an affectionate way.

Collage of Voices

I see these colonial images as a starting point for understanding my ancestry. For example, the series *Paridade* [Parity] combines the body of a person from a Central America native group with the face of someone from Maranhão or the Amazon. I think my collages provoke a historical sense of this crossing of Black and Indigenous populations. Both in the sense of awakening something related to the space of resemblance and in provoking something much more important, which is the history of these people or how two histories intersect.

After *Paridades*, I began to understand what I could produce in relation to my ancestry. I began to

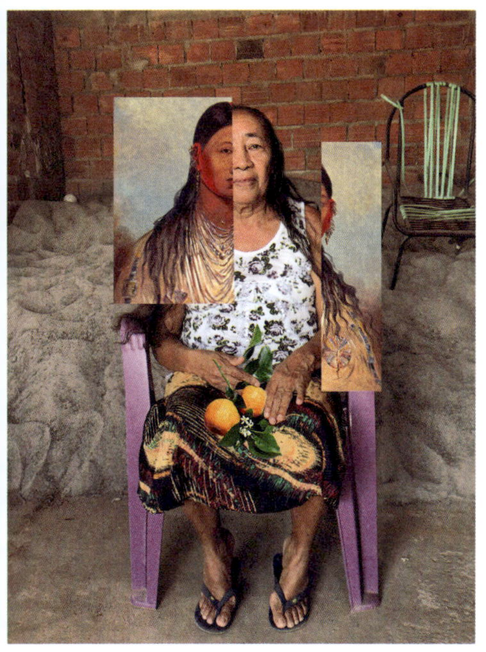

Gê Viana
Untitled *(Mantinha Marques)*, 2021
From the series *Paridade* [Parity]
Photomontage printed on
newsprint
First layer: Mantinha Marques
in Urbano Santos, Maranhão,
photographed by Gê Viana
Second layer: *Koon-za-ya-me,
Female War Eagle*, by George
Catlin (1844)
180 × 120 cm

understand the story of the woman portrayed – Dona Mantinha – and her family, and that this also has to do with the story of my family. I haven't met her family, but we're from the same people, our stories have an umbilical, historical, territorial bond, like a river that connects memories.

The term "remixing the image" stems from my experiences living with my family, who spent a good part of their lives working on a farm that provided for our own sustenance. When you plant, and you're in front of a fruit, a tree, something that is yours, that you know you planted, you can create a connection with that plant, with that territory. I think that's what my collages are, each collage is a connection, a story, a pruning, they are branches of time that I'm sewing together.

Using collage is very practical and very easy at first. But at the same time, when the research takes shape, you start to feel a certain difficulty, because you're creating a story. I'm addicted to collage. At first, I would just take the image and add other layers of images. Now it's the other way around: I think literature comes first, especially from Maranhão; I focus a lot on Maranhão's Black intellectuals, people like Mundinha, Maria Aragão, professor Carlos Benedito, and other references.

My collages connect with the temporalities of the *encantarias*,[4] the *terreiros*,[5] the *quilombos*.

A large part of what is in my collages is presented within these spaces of sociability. It's a little difficult to understand my work outside of this space, disassociated from it. People from the Tambor de Mina, Terecô, and Tambor de Crioula[6] traditions know my work and can often connect with this history. But my production is also on another level, which is a stage that only I can imagine, only I can lead, and then I create, I understand these places, these times.

I can give you a very vivid example from my practice, which is to talk about Dona Maria Dalva (Dadá), from the Santa Rosa dos Pretos *quilombo*. She once said to me: "My child, the strength of the Mina comes from the head, everything I know comes from the head." My most recent collage was created with Dadá, who is a leader of the Mina. She helped me make this collage, but it doesn't show; and yet her presence is there. When I think of ancestral technology,[7] I start from this point of spirituality, of a common, affective, and organic environment.

Radiola de promessa, which is the embryo of the work that will be shown at the Bienal, is set inside a Mina drum, because at the same time that people were moving *radiolas*,[8] there was a circle of the Caixeiras do Divino Espírito Santo, who were singing songs to the Divine. Then, at that moment, a lithograph by Debret came to mind, depicting enslaved men carrying goods for a gentleman who owned a large market in Rio de Janeiro. I couldn't wait to get home, because I really wanted to arrive and make this image; it came to me very strongly. And perhaps it has a very intense relationship with the liturgies that Maria Dalva sings. When I look at these images, I think about this presence. Who are these people who establish such a strong spiritual connection with Dadá that it makes her sing so many liturgies, so many doctrines in a single day? And could it be that Dadá's people are not the people I'm portraying? These are fabulations that I'm also creating. So these places will always give me a basis for making, creating, and telling these stories.

Sonic Memory

Music is totally present in this work at the Bienal. Dona Maria Dalva is a woman who sings a lot and carries a lot of doctrine in her head; these songs from Minas Gerais also make me think of the old masters from Casa da Mina,[9] or the African population from the kingdom of Dahomey,[10] who arrived in Maranhão with their technologies, their language, and their culture. I keep thinking about the crossover that is once again appearing here in São Luís, now with reggae. We don't speak English, we didn't know exactly what that music was, and we understood it as international music; the images didn't exist, but we recreated this music in our territory – we know how it envelops our bodies when the *radiola* plays. We can only dance close, clinging together, we can create a whole cultural and political dynamic of group resistance, which is so present in Black populations. We went round and round and round until we created a body that was very much our own, unique. Because in the 1970s there was no digital technology, no TV, no images of what was happening in Jamaica.

The *radiola* is just one element for talking about this story, because, in reality, it's the people that are the foundation of it. The making of this story is the people. When I arrived at the Mocajituba *quilombo*, in Alcântara, I realized that most of the people (from the family of dona Maria Clores)[11] who celebrate St. Benedict the Moor dance to the drum, then dance to the *radiola*, while holding a statue of the saint; these are the same people who also dance at home, receiving their entities. So I think of this time as very circular, and the *radiola* is just an instrument to make things happen in a more dignified way. The *radiola* is an economic instrument, beyond the party, the fun, the resting, and the free body. In this work for the 36th Bienal, I want to present a more intimate archival narrative.

Alcântara

During the colonial period, the city of Alcântara, in Maranhão, was economically marked by the production of cotton and sugarcane. With the decline of the big ranchers, people got together again and returned to their land, where they started this shared place. This sharing of land that has no fence, no division, is also a technology, a way of thinking. In the early 1970s, many *quilombola* communities were moved away because of the construction of the Alcântara Launch Center (CLA, in the Brazilian acronym).[12]

Even today, there is still a resistance that seeks to maintain the previous dynamic, with its rituals, its religiosity, motivated by people's desire to be on their land, since their loved ones are buried there, since the freestone is there, a specific point where people pray.

Some want the launch center there, on the grounds that it's for development. They're thinking about tourism. But others think it's not development, because how are these people going to fish? On certain days of the month, a rocket goes up, and this directly affects the tides, preventing people from getting close to the sea to fish. The technology presented there is very contradictory. And we know very well that, if the worst comes to the worst, everyone will go down, because it's a war base. But there is also the faith of Dona Miúda who says: as long as we can be here praying, saying our prayers, we will keep going.

So it's interesting to think that, while this crowd is messing around with exorbitant technology, people are in another place, with a technology of faith, of prayer, of the bush, of the spell, of blessing. There is nothing greater than our faith. I always hear from these old folks that as long as they have faith, they will continue to exist.

Beyond School

I recently realized that the images I produce are no longer mine. Of course, there is Gê Viana's authorship, but she has moved beyond this state of untouchable art. There are children cutting, chopping, re-updating my own updating. I went to Rio de Janeiro and a teacher showed me the work of a class that had made over twenty collages based on my work. I couldn't understand the scale of that in my body. That's the future. The future is made up of other people thinking and remixing things that various women are producing in collage art.

I've received invitations to include my images in textbooks and magazines, and I'm very happy with the educational aspect of my work. These textbooks are being updated, and it's nice to understand that my work has been used today to talk about this other history, because it's something I'm going to leave to my nephews, to their children. In short, it's thinking about the future of the image.

I have a teaching certification, but it just so happened that I focused more on the arts. The basis of my education was in a state school, and it's important to point that out. I studied visual arts at a federal university. When I think about technology and these new digital tools that present themselves as effective, perhaps we could call attention to the fact that this can also be harmful. I think we have to be very careful with technology. Nowadays, many children use cell phones in the classroom, and this can be good, within a pedagogical context. But how can the school organize this, to create and expand things within the institution? Another educational dynamic that I think is important to emphasize is the street itself, making art in the

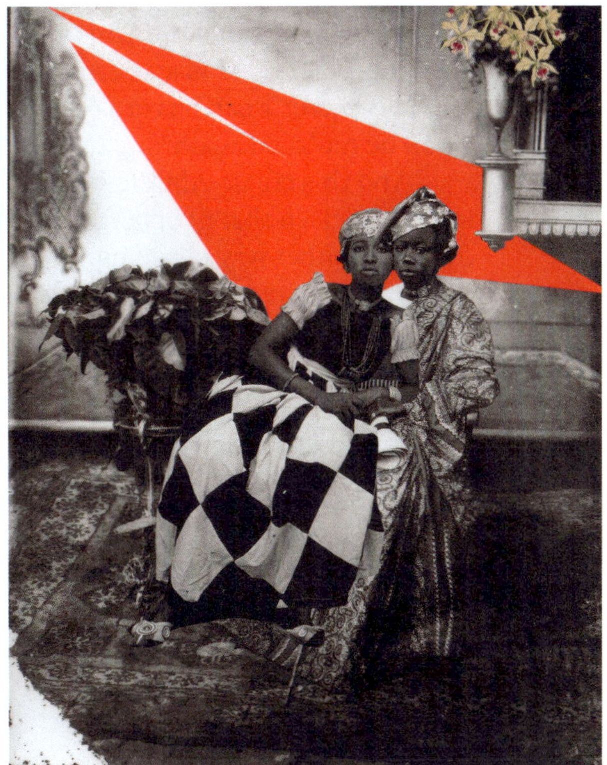

Gê Viana
Tudo que há de bonito entre nós [All the beauty between us], 2024
From the series ***Sapatona*** [Dyke]
Digital collage on *Keïta*, by Alex Agbalo
Fine art printing
100 × 80 cm
Artist's collection

street – how can teachers arrange for these students to produce and think about things outside the classroom as well?

I really like the *Sapatona* series. When I started presenting it, I felt a huge impact; sometimes I would be setting up these collages in the street and I would be approached by people. The street is an educational place; I really believe that when I put a work on the street, I'm exporting a platform for reflection to the population, whether it's a social group that already has a relationship with the subject, or a group that doesn't see itself there or whose religion doesn't accept two lesbian bodies on the street coming into contact with love, affection, and care.

One tool that is extremely important in educational work, and which I'm sure is effective, is the use of the *lambe-lambe*[13] street poster. I'm not even criticizing the idea of art inside a book, but on the street there's an impact that's public, not private, it's not the book in a classroom; these images of mine that are in books are also on the streets. So the idea is also to create a place of confrontation with those who can't deal with these images or assimilate them because of their religion beliefs. Often, in my collages, especially those in the series *Atualizações traumáticas de Debret*, people don't understand why the women are wearing clothes that resemble the garb of the Tambor de Mina (everyone wears a white cloth on their heads), and this directly affects their religiosity. So there's no better space than the street and the *lambe-lambe* to assimilate this kind of religious and gender problem, because the *lambe-lambe* is there; it can be torn off, but it can be replaced again.

And this creates different layers in the street, so that people realize there is another way of seeing. There is this other narrative, not just the narrative of my family, my religion, my church. So this is an important tool for us to think about, and I believe that using these technologies is very effective.

1   The work in question is the project commissioned for the 36th Bienal de São Paulo.

2   The series *Atualizações traumáticas de Debret* is a set of digital collages by Gê Viana that appropriates images of Brazil made in the 19th century by the French painter Jean-Baptiste Debret (1768–1848). By reinterpreting the images, the artist sought to construct new narratives based on the memories and experiences of Afro-Indigenous cultures, deconstructing scenes of colonial violence.

3   *Quilombos* are autonomous settlements historically established by runaway enslaved people (*quilombolas*) in Brazil.

4   To find out more about Maranhão's *encantarias*, see Mundicarmo Ferretti, *Maranhão encantado: encantaria maranhense e outras histórias*. São Luís: UEMA, 2000.

5   *Terreiros* are places where cults, rituals and cerimonies take place in Afro-Brazilian religions.

6   Cultural and religious manifestations of African origin that developed in the states of Pará, Amazonas, and Maranhão.

7   According to Gê Viana, technology is a broad concept, encompassing the ancestral techniques and knowledge of Black and Indigenous peoples.

8   In Maranhão, *radiolas* are large speaker systems set up like walls, used mainly to play reggae music, equivalent to the sound systems in Jamaica.

9   In the state of Maranhão, the main center for the preservation of Mina culture in Brazil, there are the Jejê (Casa das Minas) and the Nagô (Casa de Nagô) lines. Casa das Minas, founded in the second half of the 19th century, is the third *terreiro* registered with the National Historic and Artistic Heritage Institute (IPHAN) and was listed in 2002.

10   Present-day Benin.

11   Maria Clores and all the people mentioned in this text are key foundations for the construction of Gê Viana's work.

12   Located 20 miles from São Luís, the Alcântara space center was created during the military government through the appropriation of *quilombola* lands. In 2023, the Inter-American Court of Human Rights condemned the Brazilian State for violations against these communities and an Interministerial Working Group was set up to consider alternatives for demarcating the land.

13   At the 35th Bienal, the Bienal team developed the educational activity "Coreografar a palavra – lambe-lambe" [Choreographing the word – lambe-lambe]. Available at https://35.bienal.org.br/gesto-coreografar-a-palavra-lambe-lambe/. Accessed in May 2025.

Conversation with Sara Ouhaddou

Alya Sebti

Text developed from a conversation between the Fundação Bienal team, Alya Sebti (co-curator of the 36th Bienal), and the artist, held in April, 2025.

Alya Sebti: Hello, dear Sara. I wanted to interview you for this *Invocation* #4 of the 36th Bienal de São Paulo because I feel that your practice very much relates to the forms of knowledge we explored in both the first *Invocation* and in this last one.

The first *Invocation*, held in Marrakech, explored deep listening and active reception, whereas the last one, in Tokyo, looked into the "Uncanny Valley"[1] and the threshold between feeling, affectivity, and humanness.

The *Atlas Aomori* project, which you have been developing since 2018, is grounded in both places. It is situated between the Atlas Mountains, quite near Marrakech, and Aomori, a bit farther away, in Japan, which connects the work to Tokyo.

Both themes are very present in your practice. One is listening as a methodology, which is very emblematic of your collaborative approach. The other is the presence of figures created with artificial intelligence who manage to build bridges between two cultures. First, I would like to ask you what inspired you to start the *Atlas Aomori* project, connecting the Amazigh culture from the Atlas Mountains with the Jomon period of Aomori in Japan.

Sara Ouhaddou: Thank you. That is a nice question for me because it brings me back to a couple of years ago, when I had this kind of intuition. While I was traveling in southern Morocco, in the Atlas Mountains, but also in the desert, I collected all the signs and symbols I could find that had been created in the region. I wanted to know what was there even before the Amazigh culture, during prehistoric times.

I was doing this research and the following year I was invited to Japan. So I went there with a book I had created with all the drawings that were produced in Morocco during the so-called proto-historical period, when humans began to communicate using signs and symbols. Once I arrived in Japan, I began to show it to everybody I knew.

The first thing I did was to understand the history of Japan, but I quickly realized that it would be difficult to have access to its prehistoric times. I found out more about the Jomon period by questioning people on site.

It was not easy to get access to information, especially as a foreigner, but – maybe because the craft communities are wonderful human communities and we speak the same language – somehow we connected, and some of the craft communities I met in Tokyo began to show me the different places where I could see what we call

Jomon pottery. I am still studying it. And then I saw that some of the signs and symbols used on the Jomon pottery were the same as the ones I had collected from Morocco. I went even further and understood that some of the symbols had the same meanings and the same forms.

> **AS:** You said it started as an intuition, and it's something that is very present in your practice in general. We can make an interesting connection to the third *Invocation* we held, about improvisation and intuition. It also reminded me of an interview we did with the artist Tanka Fonta, who is very much outspoken about how his practice is also guided by intuition. He says it happens when you are open to the language of empathy. This is something that I see a lot in your projects, especially in this one. It's your way, I feel, to connect signs and symbols. In the end, it's only you who makes these connections. I also feel you bring this language of empathy in your everyday practice, not only in your artistic work.

SO: Well, it's nice to practice empathy, no? To acknowledge that not only intuition, but also empathy is part of what we do. I think it's the first time I've heard this, and I truly like it. Because it's true, it's only me [weaving these connections]. I always say that it is, as you know, a true fiction.

> **AS:** You start with intuition, then you build the fiction. From this fictional starting hypothesis, you create a whole methodology of collaboration. So you build, in a sense, a shared memory. Can you please elaborate on this methodology and the cartography of shared memory?

SO: Yeah, you're right. It's all linked. So, I began very naturally. I began by meeting my own family. *Voilà!* That's the basis, because they're the ones closest to me. Through them and their knowledge, and through what we share, I could open up to new communities.

Another element is the fact that I keep coming back. It can take three months or ten years, but I know, and the people I encounter and collaborate with know, that I will come back. So the trust in the continuity of the conversation is crucial. At the heart of collaboration is returning, meeting again, keeping the relationship alive, keeping in touch. I did this in Japan; I went there in 2018, and we maintained the relationship, even during covid-19. And I went back. A lot of the time you just sit and talk. But it is the most precious thing you can do: allow the time to sit and talk. That is where the intuition builds up. You nourish yourself, we all nourish ourselves, and then the thing grows.

So, at the core of my practice is the time we sit together and just talk. Then, intuitively, I began to document these moments of conversation, anywhere I go, even during my holidays, even with my parents. And at some point, after collecting so much information and so many feelings, I understood that if I wanted to make something of it for us together, or if I wanted to leave a trace somewhere for us, I needed to map it.

Honestly, if you have all those relations inside you, they eat you up. Empathy is nice, but at some point it ends up devouring your soul. You need to get it out. The only way I found to get it out was visually: it was the beginning of the mapping.

This is how, through the years, in my studio, I did those maps. I still have them, and I complete them. At some point, I send them back to the community I am collaborating with. And community doesn't mean craft communities. It can be a museum team. So, for instance, in Japan it was the museum team: I sent the map back and asked them to help me complete what I didn't know. They did, and they sent me back the map, and I have it here. This is how collaboration appears in the mapping.

AS: That's very beautiful. There is something really fascinating in your practice, not only in how you use signs and symbols, but also in how you deconstruct language, and more specifically alphabets. I think about how you've been working with such a big timespan of symbolism, based on very ancient documentation that you have brought together in the shared memory mapping, but also on the digital symbols that you explore in the video installation connected to this piece.

SO: I think it's linked to sharing everything with the people I meet and keeping the discussion alive. It also means growing with those people. In this group there are people of different ages. There are old people, kids, some that I've known since they were 10 years old, who aren't even kids anymore. And this has been very important because I saw them evolving, I saw their tools evolving, I saw their interests changing, and mine as well.

And very quickly, in our contemporary time, the digital question arises everywhere, among both the older and the younger generations, because it became part of our lives. So, from the very beginning of the project, I knew that by looking deeply at language, at how language works, I would at some point have to face technology, and digital technology.

167

In Japan it was stronger. When I studied the kanji [the Chinese ideogram system used by the Japanese] within the history of Japanese language, I quickly understood how they invented the emoji. And that's enough for an artist to think, okay, the digital question is already here.

That's also enough to make us see the connection – how human beings change their tools, but how we don't change deeply, because emojis are basically the same thing as prehistorical drawings. They are all images, only the tools are different. And it's fascinating for me, because it's all linked to craft as well. It's all linked to the handmade, and hand gesture, only the tools change. And when you change the tool, you change the shapes. This is how I see it, honestly.

The final installation of the project is called *Une Conversation Banale* [A Trivial Conversation]. It's named that way because we use all levels of language – writing, reading, digital language – every day. So, I thought, if I do an installation challenging the idea of language, challenging the idea of the alphabet rules, as politics have created them, I need to include all types of languages that exist.

The installation consists of two huts in dialogue. It's as if they were two natives, each from one region. So, one is in Morocco, in the Atlas Mountains, and the other is in Aomori. I've chosen Aomori because the craft there is very similar to the craft of the Atlas Mountains. The huts don't have an age – they have been there forever, like two stones.

So the huts are bodies that listen to and memorize their environment across time and space. And they overlap everything. That's what they do: they just overlap. At some point, by overlapping, they learn. Once they learn, they need to share. So the installation is just how a human being works.

We memorize, we learn, we share. That's what they do. But I wanted them to do it only in the spectrum of signs and symbols, as if the world, for them, had never invented the alphabets as we know them today. All of these alphabets – Arabic, Latin, even the contemporary form of kanji – are made by those signs and symbols that come from our deepest humanity. The huts work only with that, and communicate with them.

But they equip themselves with tools. And that, for me, is a way to talk about craft evolution, craft mediums, how they change through time. And it's also an experimentation to see how hybridization happens when you keep something, but change something else. So they hold on to their language, but they need to make it survive. The only way to survive is to accept the changes of their time. If they did not accept the alphabet, they had to accept technology. That's what they did to survive, to make their knowledge survive. So the huts are changing; through time,

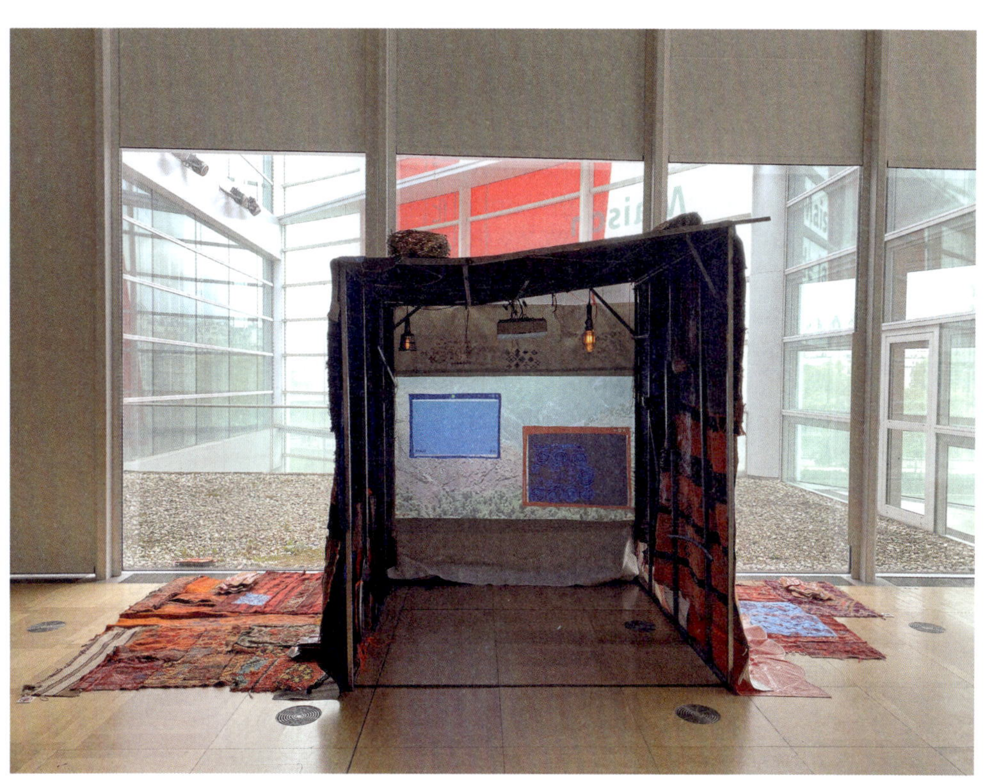

Sara Ouhaddou
Atlas-Aomori project, 2017/2022
Atlas – Une conversation banale [A trivial conversation]
Les Etres Lieux exhibition, Maison de la Culture du Japon, Paris, 2022

169

they've equipped themselves with iPhones, screens, and cameras. They film their landscape, they share it, they discuss it.

All those signs and symbols at some point became digital signs and symbols. That's how they talk today – they send each other text messages in a language they've invented. This is how it all happened to me. And the question is, how does something older survive today?

AS: For this last *Invocation* in Tokyo, the Bienal is exploring how digital figures and humanoids evoke affect, memory, eeriness, and that's why it's about the Uncanny Valley, as they mediate or represent human experience. In *Atlas Aomori*, you create bridges between distant cultures and histories through contemporary symbols.

Do you see the digital presence of these humanoid forms in your work as a way to transmit culture and memory and bridge culture across time and geographies?

SO: When I created the project and saw these humanoid figures as souls, I quickly thought that the only way for them to survive, having come from an old time, was to adapt to the new.

A major part of my practice is to deconstruct the alphabet; words or fragments of words become forms and are emptied from the meaning they carry. This experience is inspired by the story of my parents, who arrived in France without knowing the Latin alphabet and had to adapt in a world of signs that they had to accept and decipher. I try to imagine how history could have been different – what if people had the choice not to accept colonization? What if they had the choice to stick to their oral heritage? That would have been great for my parents, actually, because [it would have produced] less frustration. If they had had that choice, some other things could have happened.

You can't hold on to everything from the past, because then it means you're dead. The movement of life goes on. You have to make some changes to survive, and what are they? Here, the huts choose to adapt to the technology of their time, and I think it's an answer to ancient knowledge, and it's something I do, of course, in my everyday practice with the craft community. I think it's a way to preserve ancient knowledge.

AS: I have one wrap-up question. You said earlier that if we don't want to die, we have to adapt. There are tools that can create these bridges between cultures and, as we said, preserve and protect ancestral forms of knowledge.

My last question is more broadly about the Bienal. This edition invites us to imagine humanity as a practice and a verb – something that you conjugate every day, rather than a fixed identity. If humanity was a practice and a verb, something you commit to every day, what would your verb be, and why?

SO: Sharing. It would definitely be sharing.

1   Reference to Masahiro Mori's essay "The Uncanny Valley," which informed the 36th Bienal de São Paulo's *Invocation* #4, held in Tokyo. Available at https://spectrum.ieee.org/the-uncanny-valley. Accessed in May 2025.

Conversation with Andrew Maerkle

Thiago de Paula Souza

Conversation held by e-mail
in June, 2025.

Thiago de Paula Souza: When we began planning
Invocation #4, our starting point was the concept of the
"Uncanny Valley", coined by the late Masahiro Mori.
In "The Anxious Cyborg Manifesto" [pp. 72-86], Tavia Nyong'o
suggests that perhaps "the entire world we live in is becoming
an Uncanny Valley." Could you talk a bit about how Mori's
concept might be interpreted in 2025 and how it relates to
contemporary artistic practices? What do you see as the role of
technology for contemporary artists in the local context?

Andrew Maerkle: Masahiro Mori introduced the "Uncanny Valley" as a
metaphor to describe the sense of estrangement people feel when encoun-
tering robots that appear *too* human. He originally used the term to explain
the shape of a graph charting human emotional response to different types
of robots, so the concept essentially externalizes – or reifies – our emotions.
In that sense, I see it primarily as a tool for visualizing the dynamics of
identification and dissociation between self and other. A great deal of
othering happens unconsciously, long before we get to the overt dema-
goguery of politicians like Hitler or Trump. Recognizing that we each carry
our own uncanny valleys can help us become more aware of how we participate in discourses that seek to minimize or deny the agency of what we
perceive as foreign.

In the context of contemporary Japan, for instance, the spatial
metaphor of a "valley" is useful in thinking about the country's unresolved
imperialist legacies, which are constantly under threat of being erased by
nationalist policies of deliberate forgetting. Perhaps, as in Shiori Watanabe's
contemporary Noh play *Irumagawa* [pp. 44-47] set in a liminal zone
between life and afterlife, the Uncanny Valley even opens up a space to
summon the survivors of Japanese wartime atrocities and *speak with* them
– to borrow a phrase from bell hooks. Similarly, Asako Iwama [pp. 148-153]
taps into a temporal uncanny valley when she uses honey to evoke geno-
cides past and present – one participant told me they got goosebumps when
Iwama mentioned we were eating honey made by bees that no longer exist.

The Uncanny Valley is also a powerful image for thinking about
translation, especially as it becomes increasingly entangled with AI. We
often rely on tools like DeepL or Google Translate to gain immediate access
to texts in other languages, but these tools gloss over the intellectual labor
involved in grappling with cultural difference – precisely where translation can be most transformative. Viewed this way, the estrangement of the
Uncanny Valley that lies between languages shouldn't be avoided
but embraced for its rich potential. This is something Yūki Nagae

[pp. 122-123] explores in her contribution to the *Invocation*, when she uses machine translation to compose a poem in response to recordings of Conceição Evaristo reading in Portuguese. It also informs Tavia Nyong'o's development of Mwananchi.ai, a custom chatbot that "seeks to democratize AI by embedding it with local languages, narratives, and epistemologies."

In summary, approaching the *Invocation* through this expanded understanding of the Uncanny Valley led us to consider artistic practices that were grounded in strong thematic concerns while still touching on technological issues. I believe the program achieved a compelling synthesis of poetics, politics, and critical reflection.

TdPS: Zen and Buddhist traditions were central to Mori's articulation of the Uncanny Valley, and we know that many artists and scholars – not only in Japan but across different geographies – have been influenced by these philosophies. Do you think such traditions still play a role in contemporary artistic practices in Japan?

AM: Buddhism and Zen are deeply woven into Japanese culture, so anyone raised in a Japanese context likely has access to those traditions at some level. But for that very reason, Japanese artists are often cautious about referencing Buddhism or Zen too explicitly – it can easily slip into kitsch, reinforce patriarchal structures, or lead to reductive interpretations.

Take Mono-ha artist Kishio Suga, for example. He drew on the Buddhist philosopher Nagarjuna (c. 150–250 CE) as well as on modern thinkers like Gilles Deleuze and Maurice Merleau-Ponty in developing his sculptural "situations," which are suspended between different states of being. Yet he's careful not to directly associate his work with Buddhism in his writings. The critic, curator, and poet Shuzo Takiguchi once joked, when asked about the relationship between Duchamp and Zen, "There's nothing more dangerous for a Japanese person than to say the word *Zen*."

So there's a certain asymmetry in how Japanese and non-Japanese artists incorporate these ideas, which You Nakai touches on in his lecture-performance about John Cage and David Tudor's engagement with Japanese culture [pp. 94-105].

TdPS: Building on my previous question, in all of the *Invocations*, we've been interested in exploring possible bridges between traditional culture and contemporary practices. It has always been important for us to engage with these traditions critically – so that they don't come across as mere celebrations of symbols that, from a distance, might seem "authentic" or representative of a territory, but upon closer inspection may instead reflect caricatured views of a region or even nationalist propaganda. How do you see the involvement of artists and theorists in Tokyo, and in Japan more broadly, with elements of the country's past?

AM: This was something I gave a lot of thought to as we prepared the *Invocation*. Noh and Bunraku, for example, came up as points of reference but it's a stretch to say they exert a strong influence on contemporary expression.

Instead, poetry gradually emerged as a more vital mode of expression that bridges past and present in Japan. It offered us a continuous thread from the ancient art of Noh to the global movement of hip hop, as represented by the rappers Danny Jin and Namichie. Poetry also proved surprisingly relevant to questions around how culture is responding to new technologies. The poets were central to unpacking the "uncanny valley" theme: Natsumi Aoyagi [pp. 60-63], for instance, created a performance in collaboration with the digital assistants Alexa and Siri; Gōzō Yoshimasu [pp. 88-92] and Takako Arai read poems that reflected on histories of industry, labor, and environmental transformation across different regions of Japan; and Sakisaka Kujira [pp. 106-107] reclaimed a degree of opacity in everyday speech through her use of sign language.

Poetry also became a medium for invoking absent voices. We saw this in the pairing of Theresa Hak Kyung Cha's video *Mouth to Mouth* (1975) – in which the artist's image emerges from the static of a TV monitor to mouth the vowel sounds of the Korean language – and Cecilia Vicuña's sound installation *Rain Dreamed by Sound: Homage to Theresa Hak Kyung Cha* (2021), which honors Cha's poetic vision while mourning her violent death in 1982 at the hands of a rapist and murderer. Multiple Spirits [pp. 108-111] then contributed to that conversation by incorporating fragments of texts by Cha and Vicuña, as well as by Conceição Evaristo and Trinh T. Minh-ha, in their multilingual audio intervention into the translation headsets at Sogetsu Kaikan.

Poetry as polyphony; polymorphous poetics – its fluid, diffuse nature helped us appreciate cultural continuities that are specific to Japan, while also challenging essentialist claims to Japaneseness. It's also worth noting that the three-part structure of the *Invocation* – staged across three venues, The 5th Floor, Sogetsu Kaikan, and the University of Tokyo Komaba Campus – echoed, in some ways, the *jo-ha-kyu* structure of classical Japanese theater.

175

About the Authors

Alya Sebti is a contemporary art curator and director of the ifa-Galerie (Institut für Auslandsbeziehungen) in Berlin, where she initiated the research and exhibition platform *Untie to Tie – On Colonial Legacies in Contemporary Societies*. She was co-curator of the European biennial Manifesta in Marseille (2020), guest curator of the Dakar Biennale (2018), and artistic director of the Marrakech Biennale (2014). She has led curatorial research through mentorship programs at the ZK/U artist residency (Berlin) and at MACAAL (Marrakech).

Andrew Maerkle is a writer, editor, and translator based in Tokyo. Currently, he is the editorial director of Art Week Tokyo and a contributor to international magazines such as *frieze*, *Artforum*, and *Art & Australia*. His book of translations *Kishio Suga: Writings, vol. 2, 1980–1989* was published in 2025 by Skira. From 2010 to 2024 he was deputy editor of the online publication ART iT | International Edition. He was the deputy editor of *ArtAsiaPacific* in New York from 2006 to 2008. From 2018 to 2023 he taught at the Graduate School of Global Arts at Tokyo University of the Arts.

Anna Roberta Goetz is a curator and writer. She has worked at the Marta Herford Museum and the MMK Museum für Moderne Kunst Frankfurt. She was assistant curator and project manager of the German Pavilion at the 55th Venice Biennale (2013). She has organized major solo and group exhibitions in various countries and has taught at several international art academies, including the Zurich University of the Arts and the Städelschule in Frankfurt. Her publications include *Rodney McMillian: The Land: Not Without a Politic*, co-edited with Kathleen Rahn (2024), and *Cinthia Marcelle – By Means of Doubt*, co-edited with Isabella Rjeille (2023).

Asako Iwama is an artist based in Berlin and Tokyo. She explores the social dimensions of eating through experimental workshops and field trips. Her recent work examines historical and technological shifts in the relationship between natural elements and the body's materiality and subjectivity. She engages in practices such as casting, tracing, and collecting to reflect on these transformations. From 2005 to 2015, she worked as a cook at Studio Olafur Eliasson (Berlin), where she managed The Kitchen. She also co-created *Studio Olafur Eliasson: The Kitchen* (2013).

Bidou Yamaguchi is an artist known for creating masks used in traditional Japanese Noh theater. He stands out among the younger generation for the revitalization of traditional techniques and aesthetics that have been passed down in Japan. Trained under Noh mask maker Ogawa Gendō, he developed a profound understanding of Noh masks through his contact with a valuable collection that includes masks over 500 years old, kept by the Hōshō family.

Yamaguchi has broadened his artistic expression by creating Noh masks inspired by Western paintings in a series called "Portraits." His work is highly regarded and has been exhibited, performed, and presented in museums and universities in Japan, the United States, and the Netherlands. His pieces are held in prestigious collections, including the Rijksmuseum in Amsterdam and the Art Institute of Chicago.

Bonaventure Soh Bejeng Ndikung is a curator, author, and biotechnologist, currently serving as the director and chief curator of the Haus der Kulturen der Welt (HKW) in Berlin. He is the founder and former artistic director of SAVVY Contemporary in Berlin, as well as the artistic director of sonsbeek20→24 (Arnhem). He is a professor and head of faculty in the Master's program in Spatial Strategies at the weißensee academy of art in Berlin. His published works include, among others, *The Delusions of Care* (2021), *An Ongoing-Offcoming Tale: Ruminations on Art, Culture, Politics and Us/Others* (2022), and *Pidginization as Curatorial Method* (2023).

Deivison Faustino holds a PhD in sociology and is a professor at the School of Public Health at the University of São Paulo (USP). He has experience in teaching, research, and outreach on topics such as health and racism, digitization of health, education on ethnic-racial relations, anti-racist thinking, and capitalism and racism. He is the author of the books *Frantz Fanon: um revolucionário, particularmente negro* (2018), *Frantz Fanon e as encruzilhadas: teoria, política e subjetividade* (2022); *O colonialismo digital: por uma crítica hacker-fanoniana* (2023) e *Balanço afiado: estética e política em Jorge Ben* (2023).

Gê Viana is a visual artist trained at the Universidade Federal do Maranhão. Her practice moves between domestic and urban spaces, combining manual and digital collage, painting, and the *lambe-lambe* photographic technique. Drawing from archival imagery and her family's oral history, she constructs narratives of Afro-diasporic life in the Brazilian state of Maranhão while confronting hegemonic culture. She has participated in the Bienal das Amazônias (Belém, 2023), the 38th Panorama of Brazilian Art (Museu de Arte Moderna de São Paulo, 2024), *Histórias brasileiras* (MASP, São Paulo, 2022), and the Borås Art Biennial (2024). Her work is included in the collections of the Pinacoteca de São Paulo and the Museu de Arte Moderna do Rio de Janeiro.

Gōzō Yoshimasu is a poet and multimedia artist, a central figure of the Japanese avant-garde since the 1960s. His practice seeks to recover and reinvent the links between poetry and performance, transforming language into gesture and invention. His manuscripts operate as visual and textual collages, incorporating literary references and languages collected through travel and correspondence. He also created the *gozoCiné* series, combining video, spontaneous poetic composition, and performative reading. He has held solo exhibitions at the National Museum of Modern Art (Tokyo), Ashikaga Museum of Art, Okinawa Prefectural Museum & Art Museum (Naha), and Hokkaido University Museum (Sapporo).

Keyna Eleison is a curator, researcher, and educator in art and culture. She coordinated all public institutions from the Rio de Janeiro Municipal Department of Culture and taught at the Escola de Artes Visuais do Parque Lage, where she was also a teaching coordinator. She was the curator of the 10th Bienal Internacional de SIART in Bolivia (2018), the curator of the 1st Bienal das Amazônias (2023), the artistic director of the MAM Rio (2020–2023) and director of research and content at the Bienal das Amazônias.

Lynn Hershman Leeson is an artist and filmmaker known for her work in visual arts and cinema, exploring themes such as the relationship between humans and technology, identity, surveillance, and the use of media as a tool for empowerment against censorship and political repression. She has received numerous awards, including the SIGGRAPH Lifetime Achievement Award and the Prix Ars Electronica Golden Nica. In 2022, she received a special mention from the jury at the 59th Venice Biennale. In 2023, she was awarded an Honorary Doctorate by the Pratt Institute in New York, and the San Francisco Museum of Modern Art acquired its first NFT, created by her.

Manauara Clandestina is a visual artist and film student. Her early formation was shaped by experiences in evangelical missions in the interior of the Amazon, where she first engaged with art through church theater and music. Her practice emerges as an expression of urban nightlife and unfolds in performances that explore *travesti* (Brazilian transgender) experiences, marked by processes of transition and affectivity. She reflects on the subjectivities of dissident bodies through poetic constructions connected to the world of fashion. Her work has been shown at the Instituto de Arquitetos do Brasil and MASP (both in São Paulo), Museu de Arte Moderna do Rio de Janeiro, the Edinburgh International Film Festival, the 1st Amazon Biennial (Belém), and the 60th Venice Biennale.

Marylya is a singer/songwriter who made her debut in Los Angeles. When Japanese novelist Kenji Nakagami heard one of her concert recordings, he decided to introduce her work in Japan. Marylya has performed extensively around the world, especially in the US, Europe (France, Italy, Estonia, Greece, etc.), and Asia. She has worked with many different artists. She has collaborated several times with photographer Nobuyoshi Araki (who called her a "diva from the edge of Nirvana") and with Japanese Butoh dancer Kazuo Ohno. She has also performed extensively with Gōzō Yoshimasu around the world and in Japan (at Centre Pompidou and Bienal de São Paulo, etc.). Her work does not fit any musical category. A writer in *Option Magazine* (Los Angeles) once noted: "I don't often hear something for which I have no frame of reference."

Multiple Spirits was launched in 2018 by artist and actor Mai Endo and curator and writer Mika Maruyama. It is a bilingual art zine/magazine (in English and Japanese) dedicated to queer feminist practice. While publishing both in print and online, Multiple Spirits has served as a platform for a wide range of projects, including artistic research, exhibition-making, collaborations, talk events, and translation. These projects have highlighted art practices and activism from various perspectives by addressing intersectional issues of sexuality, gender, race, and class. In parallel, Multiple Spirits has explored art, queer feminism, and social movements in relation to publications and print culture, especially in the East Asian context and beyond.

Natsumi Aoyagi was born in 1990 in Tokyo. As a contemporary artist working with moving image media, she develops project-based works grounded in fieldwork and research. Recent activities include the solo exhibition *Logbook of a Sea Goddess* (Towada Art Center, 2022), nomination for the 7th edition of Women to Watch at the National Museum of Women in the Arts Japan [NMWA Japan] (2022), and participation in ICC Annual 2024: Faraway, so close (NTT InterCommunication Center [ICC], 2024). Her poetry collection *Done Being Nurtured* (thoasa, 2022) was awarded the 28th Nakahara Chuya Prize and was describedas a representative of the future of Japanese poetry. She also directs the art space and bookstore kohonya honkbooks.

181

Nina da Hora is a researcher in justice and artificial intelligence (AI), focusing on combating algorithmic racism. She received the title of Global Fellow from the Ford Foundation (2024), is the founder of Instituto da Hora, and holds a master's degree in Critical Artificial Intelligence from Unicamp. She serves on councils that promote responsible AI policies and innovations.

Sakisaka Kujira is a representative of Kotoba-Sha, a Japanese language school located in Okegawa City, Saitama Prefecture. In 2022, they published their first poetry collection *For a Very Small Understanding* (Shironeko-sha), and in 2023 released the first essay book *The Ideal Temperature of Love Between Couples* (Hyakumannen Shobo). Kujira contributes poems and literary reviews to local newspapers distributed by Asahi Shimbun and the news agency Kyodo Tsushinsha, as well as magazines such as *Gendai Shi Techo*.

Sara Ouhaddou is an artist living between Morocco and France. She's born in France in a Moroccan family and this dual cultural background informs her practice as an ongoing dialogueue. In her work, she balances traditional art forms with the conventions of contemporary art, aiming to place artistic creation's forgotten cultural continuities into new perspectives. She works in situ, producing works based on encounters with communities, craftsmen and researchers, while exploring heritage sites and objects. Each of her works is a project of learning, exchange of knowledge and intimate or universal stories.

Shiori Watanabe was born in Tokyo in 1984. She graduated with a degree in sculpture from Tokyo University of the Arts in 2015 and earned her MFA from the same university in 2017. Recent exhibitions include 宿/*Syuku* at Shiseido Gallery, Tokyo, in 2024; *Tototarari Tarariratarari Agarirarari To* at Shinjuku Kabukicho Noh Stage, Tokyo, in 2022; *Bebe* at Whitehouse, Tokyo, in 2021; *Non-Human Control* at Tav Gallery, Tokyo, in 2020; and *Dyadic Stem*, a two-person show with Shinjiro Watanabe at the 5th Floor, Tokyo, in 2020

T-Michael is a Ghanaian-Norwegian bespoke tailor, designer, and multidisciplinary artist whose practice interrogates the nexus of sartorial tradition and contemporary cultural discourse. Rooted in an exacting commitment to craftsmanship, his eponymous label, alongside Norwegian Rain (hyper-functional outerwear), T-Kimono (recontextualized kimonos), Film Lab, and T Creative Spaces, serves as a conduit for reimagining form, materiality, and narrative. With over 29 years of exploration, his work is a dialectic between precision and fluidity, where the poetics of construction intersect with an avant-garde ethos, challenging conventional paradigms of menswear and beyond.

Tavia Nyong'o is a critic, researcher of art and performance and the William Lampson Professor of American Studies at Yale University. His work in critical theory and performance studies explores the intersection of history, imagination, and Black aesthetic life through the lens of performance. His award-winning books include *The Amalgamation Waltz: Race, Performance, and the Ruses of Memory* (University of Minnesota Press, 2009), *Afro-Fabulations: The Queer Drama of Black Life* (New York University Press, 2018) and *Black Apocalypse: Afrofuturism at the End of the World* (University of California Press, 2025). Currently curating public programs at the Park Avenue Armory, Nyong'o is completing groundbreaking research on topics ranging from digital technology's cultural history to racial and sexual dissidence in art and culture.

Thiago de Paula Souza is a curator and educator. He was co-curator of the 38th Panorama of Brazilian Art at MAM São Paulo (2024), the exhibition *Some May Work as Symbols: Art Made in Brazil, 1950s–70s* at Raven Row

(London), the Nomadic Program at Vleeshal Center for Contemporary Art (Middelburg) between 2022 and 2023, *While We Are Embattled*, at Para Site, Hong Kong), and *Atos de Revolta* (MAM Rio) in 2022. Between 2020 and 2021, he was part of the curatorial team for the 3rd edition of Frestas – Trienal de Artes (São Paulo). He served as curatorial advisor for the 58th Carnegie International (2021–2022). From 2018 to 2019, he curated Tony Cokes' first solo exhibition at BAK (Utrecht). He was also part of the curatorial team of the 10th Berlin Biennale (2018). He is currently a member of the Artistic Committee of the NESR Art Foundation in Angola and is a PhD candidate in the arts program at HDK-Valand – University of Gothenburg.

You Nakai makes music(ians), dance(rs), haunted musical mansions, nursery rhymes, and other forms of performances as a member of No Collective, and publishes experimental children's books written by children and other literary oddities as a member of Already Not Yet. As a scholar, he has been conducting extensive research on David Tudor, the results of which have been published as *Reminded by the Instruments: David Tudor's Music* (Oxford University Press, 2021). Recent artistic endeavors include bringing to life – after a 50-year hiatus – the once-unfinished project

"Island Eye Island Ear," a speculative plan conceived by Tudor in the mid-1970s to turn an entire island into a giant musical instrument. You is currently affiliated with the University of Tokyo, where he engages in performative research on the notion of influence, teaches courses on Fake Western Music History and Pseudo-history of Experimental Music, hosts the Side Effects Lab of the University of Tokyo, and chairs the Department of Avant-garde Arts.

Yūki Nagae is a poet and writer who views poetry not just as a textual form but also as an action. Based on a concept of "poetry in action" that employs everything from digital media to water and other natural materials as her poetic mediums, Nagae proposes new ways of viewing and perceiving the world by deconstructing the environment and society through a poetic gaze and then reconstructing them through technology. She has presented her work at events across Japan and beyond, including the Centre Pompidou–organized Jonas Mekas Poetry Day (2024), and has also curated projects including "The Touch of the City on the Skin of Poetry" (2022). Her book of poems *Fuzai Toshi* won the Rekitei Prize in 2019, and her book of fiction *Jisuberi* was nominated for the 2025 Akutagawa Prize.

Fundação Bienal de São Paulo – Team

Superintendencies

Antonio Thomaz Lessa Garcia Junior · *chief operating officer*

Felipe Isola · *chief projects officer*
Joaquim Millan · *chief projects officer*

Caroline Carrion · *chief communications officer*

Irina Cypel · *chief institutional relations and partnerships officer*

Executive Superintendency
assistants
Beatriz Reiter Santos · *executive assistant*
Marcella Batista · *administrative assistant*

Projects Superintendency
Production
coordinators
Bernard Lemos Tjabbes
Dorinha Santos
Marina Scaramuzza
producers
Ariel Rosa Grininger
Camilla Ayla
Carolina da Costa Angelo
Nuno Holanda Sá do Espírito Santo
Tatiana Oliveira de Farias
assistants
Fabiana Paulucci
Ziza Rovigatti

Communications Superintendency
coordinator
Rafael Falasco · *editorial*
advisors
Adriano Campos · *design*
Eduardo Lirani · *graphic production*
Fernando Pereira · *press office*
Francisco Belle Bresolin · *digital projects and documentation*
Julia Bolliger Murari · *social media*
Luciana Araujo Marques · *editorial*
Nina Nunes · *design*
assistant
Marina Fonseca · *social media*
apprentice
Victória Pracedino

Institutional Relations and Partnerships Superintendency
advisors
Luciana Raele
Raquel Silva
Victória Bayma
Viviane Teixeira
assistants
André Massena
Jefferson Faria
Laura Caldas

Education
manager
Simone Lopes de Lira
coordinator
Danilo Pera

advisors
André Leitão
Renato Lopes
Tailicie Nascimento
assistants
Gabri Gregorio
Giovanna Endrigo
Julia Iwanaga
Vinicius Massimino
apprentice
Lincon Amaral

Bienal Archive
manager
Leno Veras
coordinators
Antonio Paulo Carretta
Marcele Souto Yakabi
assistants
Ana Helena Grizotto Custódio
Anna Beatriz Corrêa Bortoletto
Daniel Malva Ribeiro
Gislene Sales
Gustavo Paes
Kleber Costa Timoteo
Raquel Coelho Moliterno
Thais Ferreira Dias
apprentices
Ilana Alionço
Manoel Assis

**Financial and Administrative
Finances**
manager
Amarildo Firmino Gomes
coordinator
Edson Pereira de Carvalho
advisor
Fábio Kato
assistant
Silvia Andrade Simões Branco

Materials and Property
manager
Valdomiro Rodrigues da Silva Neto
coordinators
Larissa Di Ciero Ferradas · *materials
and property*
Vinícius Robson da Silva Araújo ·
purchasing
assistants
Angélica de Oliveira Divino
Daniel Pereira
Sergio Faria Lima
Victor Senciel
Wagner Pereira de Andrade
auxiliary
Isabela Cardoso
apprentice
Lucas Galhardo

Planning and Operations
advisors
Rone Amabile
Vera Lucia Kogan

Human Resources
coordinators
Andréa Moreira · *human resources*
Higor Tocchio · *payroll and
personnel department*
assistants
Matheus Andrade Sartori
Patricia Fernandes

Information Technology
consultants
Ricardo Bellucci
Júlio Coelho
Matheus Lourenço
assistant
Jhones Alves do Nascimento

**36ª Bienal de São Paulo –
*Not All Travellers Walk Roads
– Of Humanity as Practice***

Conceptual Team
Bonaventure Soh Bejeng Ndikung ·
 chief curator
Alya Sebti, Anna Roberta Goetz,
 Thiago de Paula Souza · *co-curators*
Keyna Eleison · *co-curator at large*
Henriette Gallus · *strategy and
 communications advisor*
André Pitol, Leonardo Matsuhei ·
 curatorial assistants

**Architecture and Exhibition
Design**
Gisele de Paula, Tiago Guimarães
Alexandra Souza, Santiago Rid ·
 architectural assistance
Agence Clémence Farrell ·
 initial architectural advisory

Visual Identity
Studio Yukiko

**Projects and Production
Acoustic Advisory**
Alexandre Sresnewsky

Assembly Coordination
Alexandre Cruz
Arão Nunes
Mauro Amorim

Audiovisual Advisory
Patrícia Mesquita

Conservation
coordination
Patrícia Guimarães dos Reis

team
Alice Quintella Tischer
Daniel Zuim Mussi
Ellen Marianne Röpke Ferrando
Fabiana Franco Barbosa Oda
Gisele Guedes
Thaís Ramos Carvalhais
Valerie Midori Koga Takeda

Fine Arts Insurance
Sonia Sassi

Public Program Production
Helena Prado

Transportation Logistcs
Nilson Lopes · *national*
Waiver Arts · *international*

**Communications and Editorial
AV Content and Photographic
Documentation**
Bruno Fernandes
Duma Hub de Inovação Criativa e
 Produção Artística
João Gabriel Hidalgo

Design Assistance
Aninha de Carvalho Price
Tamara Lichtenstein

Editorial
Cristina Fino · *editorial
 coordination of the educational
 publications #3 / #4*
Deborah Moreira · *editorial
 assistance*

Press Office
Index · *national press office*
Sam Talbot · *international press office*

Website
Fluxo

Invocations

Marrakech – Nov 14-15, 2024
LE 18 · *co-convener*
Laila Hida · *partner venue direction*
Youssef Sebti · *local production*
Zora El Hajji · *local press office*
Mahacine Mokdad, Sofian
 Amly, Hamza Morchid, Youssef
 Boumbarek · *AV content and
 photographic documentation*
Embaixada do Brasil em Rabat
 / Instituto Guimarães Rosa
 · Ministério das Relações
 Exteriores – *local support*

Guadeloupe – Dec 5-7, 2024
Lafabri'K · *co-convener*
Marie-Laure Poitout · *partner venue
 presidency*
Léna Blou · *partner venue direction*
Hellen Rugard · *local production*
Annik Benjamin · *simultaneous
 translation*
Cédric Marcellin, Philippe Hurgon –
 *AV content and photographic
 documentation*
Institut Français; Embaixada
 do Brasil em Paris / Instituto
 Guimarães Rosa · Ministério das
 Relações Exteriores · *local support*

Zanzibar – Feb 11-13, 2025
Bernard Ntahondi · *co-convener*
Dhow Countries Music Academy
 (DCMA) · *partner institution*
Halda Alkanaan · *partner institu-
 tion direction*

Thureiya Saleh · *local production*
Raymond Peter, Alex Marcel –
 sound engineering
William Chazega Nkobi,
 Habibu Ramadhani Diliwa · *simul-
 taneous translation*
Aden Rajab Said, Ally Nassor,
 Arafat Khamis Moh'd, Caroline-
 Jamie Dandu, Gulaam Abdullah,
 Venance Leonard, Waleed Khamis
 Mohammed · *AV content and
 photographic documentation*
YAS, Fondation H, Embaixada do
 Brasil em Dar es Salaam / Instituto
 Guimarães Rosa · Ministério das
 Relações Exteriores · *local support*

Tokyo – Apr 12-14, 2025
Andrew Maerkle, Kanako
 Sugiyama – *co-convener*
The 5th Floor; Sogetsu Kaikan;
 The University of Tokyo (with
 ACUT) · *venues*
Jordan A. Y. Smith · *poetry program
 advising*
Tomoya Iwata · *local production*
Yoshiko Kurata · *local press office*
Wataru Shoji · *sound engineering*
Art Translators Collective · *simulta-
 neous translation*
Kenji Agata, Naoki Takehisa, Sora
 Shirai, Takuma Osugi, Yoshikatsu
 Hirayama · *AV content and photo-
 graphic documentation*
Embaixada do Brasil em Tóquio
 / Instituto Guimarães Rosa ·
 Ministério das Relações Exteriores;
 Art Center, The University of
 Tokyo (ACUT) · *local support*

Educational Publication #4

Edited by
Conceptual team and Fundação
 Bienal de São Paulo

Published by
Fundação Bienal de São Paulo
 and Center for Art, Research and
 Alliances (CARA), in Portuguese
 and English

Design
Studio Yukiko

Editorial coordination
Cristina Fino

Graphic production
Fundação Bienal de São Paulo

Layout
Aninha de Carvalho Price

Editorial assistance
Deborah Moreira

Copyediting and proofreading
Bruno Rodrigues, Richard Sanches,
 Tatiana Allegro

Translation
Alexandre Barbosa de Souza,
 Mariana Nacif Mendes,
 Philip Somervell

Font families
Arizona and Camera Plain
 by Dinamo

Printing
Ipsis

ISBN
978-1-954939-14-1

Distributed worldwide by
ARTBOOK | D.A.P.
75 Broad Street, Suite 630
New York, NY 10004
orders@dapinc.com
www.artbook.com

This book was published in
Portuguese and English in June
2025, as part of the project of the
36th Bienal de São Paulo.

The title of the 36th Bienal de
São Paulo, *'Not All Travellers Walk
Roads'*, is made up of verses by the
writer Conceição Evaristo

Fundação Bienal de São Paulo
Av. Pedro Álvares Cabral – Moema
04094-050 / São Paulo – SP
bienal.org.br

Center for Art, Research and Alliances (CARA)
225 West 13th Street
New York, NY 10011
cara-nyc.org

Cataloging in Publication (CIP)

Bukimi No Tani (不気味の谷): The Uncanny Valley –
    The Affectivity of the Humanoid:
    educational publication: vol. 4 /
    edited by Fundação Bienal de São Paulo;
    curated by Bonaventure Soh Bejeng Ndikung. -- São Paulo:
    Bienal de São Paulo, 2025.

ISBN 978-1-954939-14-1

1. Art – São Paulo (State) – Exhibitions
2. Bienal de São Paulo (SP)
3. Culture
4. Education
5. Mediation

I. Fundação Bienal de São Paulo.
II. Ndikung, Bonaventure Soh Bejeng.

25-273124   CDD-709.8161

Systematic Catalog Index:
Art Biennials: São Paulo: City 709.8161

Antonio Paulo Carretta – Librarian – CRB-8/6084

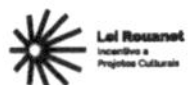 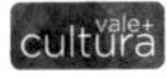 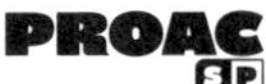

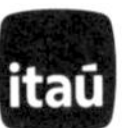

strategic partnership

master sponsorship

Bloomberg 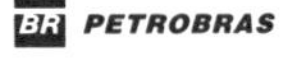 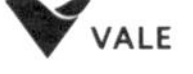 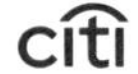

sponsorship

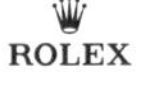 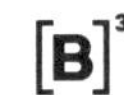

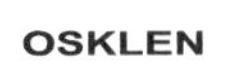 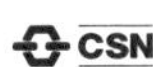 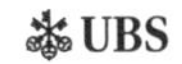 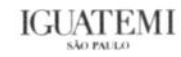  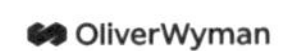 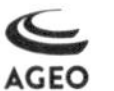 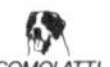 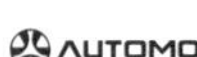  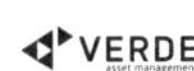   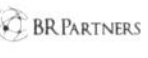  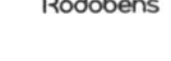 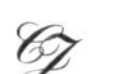 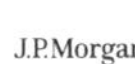

support

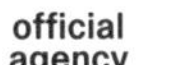  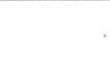 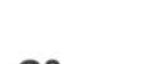 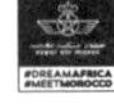 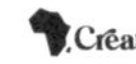  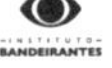 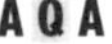 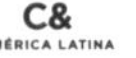 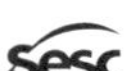

<table>
<tr><td>official
carrier</td><td>official
agency</td><td colspan="3">midia support</td><td>cultural
partnership</td></tr>
</table>

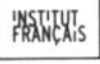 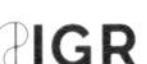 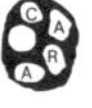 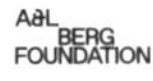 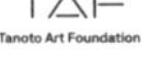 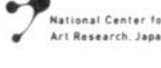

international support

 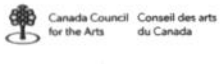 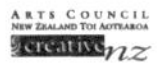 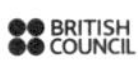 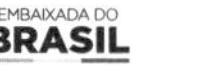 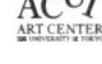

local support

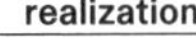

<table>
<tr><td>institutional
support</td><td colspan="6">realization</td></tr>
</table>

 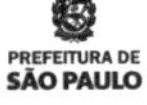 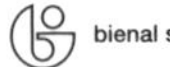 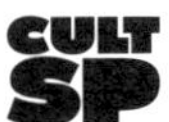 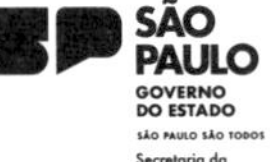 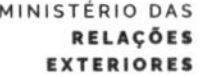 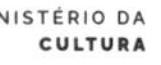 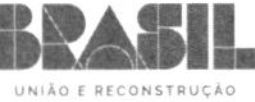